$22.95
642 Sarich, John
SAR Entertaining simply
11/06 : creating seasonal

THE BRUMBACK LIBRARY
OF VAN WERT COUNTY
VAN WERT, OHIO

# *Entertaining* SIMPLY

*Creating seasonal parties when there's no time!*

John Sarich *and* Diana Dillard

642 SAR

## *Dedications:*

*This book is for my family and friends who have entertained me so much over the years, and whom I've had the pleasure of entertaining in turn. May this remind us all of the great times we have getting together and help us do it a little more often. Let these ideas enhance our parties, and lighten our lives.*

—JOHN SARICH

*I wish to dedicate this first book of mine to my husband, Tom, who continually supports and encourages me in all my endeavors. Befittingly also, because it was our common passion for food that brought us together many years ago. And to the two most incredible little dishes I have EVER created, Hanna and Ellie. I also wish to express my gratitude to all the folks at Sea-Hill Press for presenting me with the fabulous opportunity to write this book.*

—DIANA DILLARD

PUBLISHER: Greg Sharp
EDITOR-IN-CHIEF: Cynthia Sharp
EDITORIAL ASSISTANT: Jamie Trubia
ART DIRECTOR: Barbara Schmitt
PRODUCTION ASSISTANT: Heather Bauerle
ILLUSTRATOR: Kelly Jackson
PHOTOGRAPHER: Christopher Conrad
PHOTOGRAPHY ASSISTANT: Isobel Alexander
FOOD STYLISTS: John Sarich, Diana Dillard, and Lynne Vea

Published by Sea-Hill Press, Inc.
6101 200th St. SW, Suite 205
Lynnwood, WA 98036
425.697.3606
www.seahillpress.com

All recipes include American and metric measurements. Metric conversions are written for ease of use and are not exact; they are based on a standard developed for this book.

ISBN 0-9708050-1-2
Sarich, John and Dillard, Diana
Entertaining Simply: Creating seasonal parties when there's no time.

All Rights Reserved. ©Sea-Hill Press, Inc.
This book, or parts thereof, may not be reproduced in any form without permission.

10 9 8 7 6 5 4 3 2 1

Printed in Hong Kong

# *Table of Contents*

# *Gourmet Entertaining*

*I*'ve spent years cooking for others, and my favorite thing to do is to cook for friends and family. I've been putting together parties, dinners, and buffets for so long that it's become second nature, and because of that I often get asked how you can put together a delicious and fun party without pulling your hair out. In other words, how to entertain simply.

*John Sarich*

We decided to create this book to make it easy and fun to entertain. Diana's expertise and organizational skill really shine in the planning charts provided for each menu. One of the great things about this book is that it takes the last-minute rushing out of your party preparation. You can make many of these recipes days in advance, and what you do have to do on the day of the party is clearly laid out. And while we do simplify entertaining, we don't dumb-down our recipes. Part of the joy of giving a fantastic party is in the food itself, in both cooking it and eating it.

We've created some wonderful seasonal menus with recipes that incorporate all that is fresh and delicious in each season. If you've never had a picnic in December, you'll surely be looking for an excuse to have one after looking at what we've got planned. There are plans for everything from traditional sit-down meals to informal dessert buffets. And while recipes are planned for eight guests, you can easily cut the menus in half or multiply them to serve as few as four or as many as sixteen. You set your own limits with this book.

Making what you drink as pleasurable as what you eat is an important component of party planning, and that isn't forgotten here. Each menu comes with appropriate beverage suggestions to make beverage planning simple. When planning a large party with multiple recipes, it can be difficult to decide which wines are appropriate to serve, and we give a few ideas for each menu.

When all of the planning and cooking is done, we want you to enter your own party ready to enjoy what you've created. Relaxing to share your gourmet meal with your guests is the best part of the party, and we make that easier to do with this book.

# When There's No Time

Between us, John and I have hosted thousands of parties both professionally and personally.

Hospitality involves taking care of people, nurturing them and making them feel good. A good host or hostess looks after the comfort of their guests—concerning themselves with their surroundings.

I have learned how to throw a successful party by making many mistakes. My biggest errors were made from improper planning. Even as a professional chef, I would find myself scurrying around the kitchen throughout my entire party. My guests seemed to always have a great time, however when they left I realized that I hadn't spent any time chatting with them or enjoying the food I had slaved over for days! Hence, we bring you *Entertaining Simply*.

Oh, how I wish I had practiced this type of organization and planning years ago when I first started entertaining! Our hope is that it takes the stress out of your planning and allows you time to enjoy both the food and the conversation with your guests.

We have included cooking tips, equipment suggestions, and beverage ideas throughout the book along with fabulous recipes. The teacher in me hopes you will enjoy learning about the value of using quality ingredients in your cooking. In addition to John's expert wine selections we have included non-alcoholic beverage ideas as well. Remember, relax, have fun, and enjoy... it's your party!

*Diana Dillard*

# Guidelines For Entertaining Simply

It's not the cooking that makes us all procrastinate on setting a date for our next party—it's the planning and organizing!

The aim of *Entertaining Simply* is to help eliminate that sense of being overwhelmed. We want you to sleep at night undisturbed by any worries about your upcoming event.

Look at the planning guide as a step-by-step "to-do list" that will keep you organized and on schedule, but don't let it make you panic. Do what you can each day and always look ahead to understand your timing. The shopping list at the end of each menu section provides a complete list of ingredients so that you can clearly see what you need to buy. Remember to check your pantry first!

Following are some party tips and ideas that we have found helpful in planning and enjoying the hosting of a terrific party.

**HOSPITALITY:**

GETTING HELP Though we've written the book for one person, you can easily share the workload. Start your own party club—it can be a lot of fun to have everyone bring one dish on the menu. Or, split the menu and the work with one friend. At the very least, you can always ask guests to bring along an appropriate wine or beverage.

DIRECTIONS Providing directions over the phone is okay in a pinch but written directions, especially a map, are certainly preferable. If you have the creative urge and the time, draw your own personalized map. If not, you'll find the Internet a great source to go to for a printed map and directions. Another great way is to photocopy a map of your local area and embellish it with your own details.

INVITATIONS Have fun with invitations and play it up! The joy of a marvelous party begins with your own enthusiasm. Generally, you'll be inviting guests three days to three weeks before the party. Yes, it's OK to suggest a babysitter. There are many informal occasions where a simple phone call is all that's required. Certainly an impromptu gathering can be fun, but for these menus do try to give yourself at least four days to prepare. It will make all the difference in creating an organized and relaxed party. Invitations should include the day, date, and time, of course, as well as RSVP details and any special information for your guests.

NEIGHBORHOOD Notify your neighbors before the party. Plan your parking arrangements. If you're expecting a noisy crowd, the best bet may be to invite your neighbors along to enjoy the occasion.

PLACE CARDS What a wonderful way to bring yourself into the mood of a party! Writing out place cards forces you to think of your guests' personalities and reminds you what a party is really all about—the people! Place cards can provide decorations as well, and can be matched to your theme. They also play a practical role. You won't have to stop and think before you answer that question, "Where would you like me to sit?" Instead, you'll be focused on making your guests comfortable and showing them to their seats.

## SHOPPING:

BEVERAGES See page 10 for a discussion of wine, beer and liquor selections. In addition, provide 3 cans of soda or non-alcoholic drinks per person. It's always appropriate to offer coffee for brunches, formal dinners, and dessert buffets. Provide water or juice in attractive pitchers for your guests.

GROCERY STORES Most of the ingredients you'll find at your regular local grocery store, though there may be a few ingredients you haven't used previously. We've put in tips to help you find these either in your local store or specialty market. Don't wait till the last minute to shop for these; try to scout out your specialty stores early in the planning stage.

PERIMETER SHOPPING Stay out of the center of the store as much as possible! The freshest food is on the outside of most grocery stores. The temptation to buy items you don't need will be greatest on the ends of the aisles, so look away and stick to your list! To save time, don't walk up and down the aisles. To save money, stick to your list.

QUANTITIES You'll need to calculate the number of napkins, wine glasses, and beverage glasses to put out as well as the amount of food and drink to provide. Plan for 4 cocktail napkins and 2 dinner napkins per person. You'll probably need 2 to 3 wineglasses, and 2 beverage glasses per person. As far as food goes, these menus will help you with that.

## FOOD PREPARATION:

FOOD SAFETY Use chafing dishes to keep food warm. Make an ice bath for the serving bowls holding cold food.

GARNISHING A delicious dish really shows itself when properly garnished with a sprinkle of herbs, edible flowers, the addition of lemon or lime and sprouts, a colorful tomato wedge or kumquat. Take the time to add finishing touches.

GREENS If you buy the seasonal mix of greens that the store sells by the pound it should already be clean of dirt and grit. If you do wash your greens, be careful, for they are a delicate mix and will bruise easily. Use paper towels to absorb moisture.

POSITIONING FOOD To avoid last-minute confusion, use sticky-notes to label what will go into each bowl, platter, and basket as well as labeling their position on the table or buffet.

SUBSTITUTING Ingredients as well as entire dishes on the menu can be substituted. Don't hesitate to do so if your guests' preferences or health issues dictate changes. Nuts are one of the most common of all food allergies or risks. In most recipes in this book, there's a recommended substitute.

**STAGING:**

BUFFET IDEAS Organize your buffet for the greatest efficiency. Roll flatware into napkins and place in a basket or bowl at the end of the serving line. This way guests don't have to juggle them in their hands while they try to fill their plates. Place dinner plates at the beginning of the serving line, covered with a towel to keep clean. Set up similar dishes near each other—salads with salads, main dishes with mains. For dramatic effect, place objects under your tablecloth to serve as pedestals for displaying the food. Telephone books, paint cans, boxes, bowls and dishes turned upside down, and round buckets or cookie tins all work well.

CLEANING Always try to clean as you cook. Prioritize. You can always continue cooking once your guests arrive, but you can't keep cleaning, so clean early. Table setting, presentation, and ambiance are the first things your guests will notice. Have a place ready for coats; a cleared out closet or on a bed will do. Have sparkling sinks and toilets, and ample toilet paper, soap, and towels in the bathroom, as you don't want to be taking care of these things during the party. If you can't get to the whole house, dim the lights and light the candles!

COFFEE AND TEA Set up a coffee and tea bar by placing sugar (cubes, colored crystals, vanilla, and raw sugar all make terrific displays), creamer, and spoons on a serving tray before guests arrive. Whipped cream, shaved chocolate, and cinnamon give it pizzazz. Add lemon wedges and an assortment of teas.

DECORATIONS Simple and seasonal decorations are best. Put the menu in a frame and display it for your guests. Float candles in your bathtub. Little food labels near each serving dish can be a lovely way to let your guests know what is being served and add a touch of either whimsical or elegant decoration, too.

SPRING/SUMMER Hunt in your garden for small, colorful wildflowers to scatter between the platters. Pussy willows, apple blossoms, and forsythia branches make beautiful seasonal displays. Decorate your buffet table with a display of cherries or fresh berries.

FALL/WINTER Use apples, gourds, a hollowed squash with a candle placed inside, colorful autumn leaves, an assortment of fresh peppers, and mason jars as flower vases. Red and green peppers, evergreen branches tied with a colorful ribbon, pinecones left natural or sprayed with gold or glitter are great choices.

GIFTS Gifts at the table for a formal dinner are always a nice touch. Spiced Walnuts and Pecans and Cured Olives (page 64) are two favorites. Tiny boxes of chocolates or little wrapped gifts look beautiful.

SCENTS Before your guests arrive for your fall or winter buffet party, simmer apple cider with a few cinnamon sticks. Your house will be filled with a warm and inviting aroma, and the cider can be offered to your guests as they arrive.

TIMING THE PRESENTATION Staggering the presentation at your hors d'oeuvres or dessert party can be a great feature. Rather than bringing it all out at once, your guests will be interested to see what new items have arrived on the serving buffet. This allows them to enjoy each dish.

TRASH AND RECYCLING Have recycling bins set out, know where the dirty cups, glasses, and plates will go before the party begins. Be sure to take a trash bag on your picnic. The drink area will be littered with most of the napkins and empty glasses, so have a bin nearby. You may want to lay a drop cloth beneath the drink area to prevent spills from ruining your floor. Plan a designated smoking spot somewhere near the party place, and remember the ashtrays.

TROUBLESHOOTING You can plan, prepare, and check the details, but something could still surprise you. If a guest is inebriated, you must call a taxi or arrange for a safe ride home. If there's an unexpected arrival at the door or a phone call that interrupts the meal, make good choices and don't neglect your guests. If the food burns, there's always delivery, and a future story to tell! Too much salt: add potatoes, then remove before serving. There are solutions to everything, so keep a level head and move forward!

# *Food And Wine*

*John Sarich*

I come from a typical Mediterranean family, where when you threw a party and didn't have enough leftover food for everyone to bring home a full meal, then you didn't make enough food. Most people follow a more conservative guide, and I would recommend purchasing about a half a pound of raw meat per guest, and a third of a pound raw fish per guest (less shrinking occurs with fish).

When buying beverages for your party, think about whom you've invited. While I've recommended wines with all menus and beer when appropriate, if you've got a beer-drinker buddy or a red wine-only friend, have their favorites on hand to be gracious. Keep your guests in mind when purchasing alcohol, too: buy about a half a bottle per person, and a bottle and a half of beer each for beer drinkers. It averages out so that you can avoid over-pouring anyone, but do keep an eye on your party and always call a cab or arrange a ride home for someone who has drunk too much. Remember to have an attractive selection of tonic, soda water or sparkling mineral water, soft drinks and juice available.

For a formal occasion, you'll want to either sneak down to your cellar to dust off a few bottles you've been saving, or purchase a better wine, such as one from a single vineyard or a reserve. For other events, when you'd rather economize, there are many wines in the $10 to $15 range that offer quality with value. It can be difficult to chose a wine when serving lots of different dishes, such as with an hors d'oeuvres or buffet party. But that can also be part of the fun—offer several varieties, and make the wine as much a part of the event as the food. Just keep in mind the general guide that full wines taste best with full dishes, and light food goes great with light wine.

Keep in mind appropriate serving temperatures for wine. If a white wine has been refrigerated, move it from the refrigerator 20 minutes before serving to release its bouquet. Conversely, red wine should be served at a cellar temperature of 64°F to 66°F—not room temperature. On a hot day you might want to chill your reds for 20 minutes in the refrigerator before serving. When serving sparkling wine, the proverbial ice bucket is wonderful. It provides a nice display and keeps the bubbly ice cold, as it should be.

Make your decorations simple, uncluttered, and seasonal. Less is more, and let the attention rest on your food, wine, and friends.

# *fall/winter brunch*

fall and winter are ideal times for entertaining because of the many holidays and activities that take place. An opportunity to entertain that can be easily overlooked is brunch, and a fall/winter brunch can be perfect on a cold day. Think of a blustery mid-morning, and an informal gathering of friends before a fire. Conversation flows smoothly over the delightful and unique tastes of this menu.

The recipes will fill your house with wonderful aromas and your guests with warming foods. Your guests will love the sweet to savory balance in this menu. They will find themselves completely satiated with Roasted Poblano Chile and Sausage Strata and Mushroom Tart. Fresh Greens with Shallot-Lemon Vinaigrette nicely rounds out the menu by providing an assertive contrast. Apple-Butternut Squash Soup and Sweet Potato Muffins with Maple Butter provide just the right amount of sweetness without leaving your guests craving a sugary finale.

This menu just screams for sparkling wine. There are three main types of sparkling wine, based on how sweet they are. Blanc de blancs are the driest, or least sweet, of the sparkling wines. Brut is less dry, and the sweetest is called extra dry. It can be a bit confusing when looking at labels, so keep these designations in mind when heading to the store.

For this particular menu, if you like you can serve your guests an extra dry sparkling wine as they arrive, and serve a blanc de blanc or a brut sparkling wine along with the meal. For a still wine, Chardonnay would work very well with these flavors.

FALL/WINTER

# *Brunch Menu*

*Sweet Potato Muffins*

*Maple Butter*

PAGE 16-17

*Apple-Butternut Squash Soup*

PAGE 18

*Roasted Poblano Chile*

*and Sausage Strata*

PAGE 19

*Mushroom Tart*

PAGE 20

*Fresh Greens with*

*Shallot-Lemon Vinaigrette*

PAGE 21

BEVERAGE SUGGESTIONS

*Sparkling Wines*

*or Chardonnay*

*Apple/Sparkling Apple Juice*

*Coffee Varietal (Sumatra)*

*Photo: Roasted Poblano Chile and Sausage Strata*

# Brunch *planning guide*

| | **ADVANCE PREPARATIONS** | **PREP TIME** *(2 to 3 Days Ahead)* |
|---|---|---|
|   | ▪ Create guest list. Call or send invitations. Provide directions if needed.<br>▪ Print shopping list & menu from www.seahillpress.com website. | ▪ Call any guests who have not responded.<br>▪ Talk to neighbors & plan parking arrangements. |
|   | ▪ Review shopping list and check your staples.<br>▪ Purchase ingredients for Maple Butter. | ▪ Purchase beverages & groceries. |
|   | ▪ Make Maple Butter up to one week in advance. Pipe into rosettes if desired. Freeze. | ▪ Cook sweet potato & purée for muffins. Refrigerate.<br>▪ Make Apple-Butternut Squash Soup. Refrigerate.<br>▪ Roast, peel, & chop poblano chiles for strata. Refrigerate.<br>▪ Toast almonds for soup & store at room temperature in airtight container. |
|   | ▪ Clean & organize refrigerator.<br>▪ Sketch a diagram of seating plan, table set-up, & placement of items.<br>▪ Plan & purchase tableware & decorations.<br>▪ Borrow or purchase needed cookware & serving dishes.<br>▪ Schedule childcare if needed.<br>▪ Decide what to wear. | ▪ Gather, wash, & polish serving platters, utensils, dishes, & glassware.<br>▪ Cover all items with plastic wrap or tablecloth to keep clean. |

*Much of your cooking and preparation is best done the day before this brunch, so plan to set aside that day to cook and clean. These are just guidelines to help your party go as smoothly as possible. Remember that you are not bound to follow these timelines precisely. Have fun!*

| DAY BEFORE EVENT | DAY OF EVENT | LAST TWO HOURS |
|---|---|---|
| | ▪ Assist guests with last-minute questions & requests. | |
| | ▪ Purchase last-minute items: ice, flowers. | |
| ▪ Prepare & bake crust for Mushroom Tart. Store loosely covered at room temperature.<br>▪ Slice mushrooms for tart. Refrigerate.<br>▪ Cut chives for soup, mince for greens.<br>▪ Grate cheese for strata. Refrigerate.<br>▪ Cook sausage for strata. Refrigerate.<br>▪ Make vinaigrette.<br>▪ Pull Maple Butter from freezer to refrigerator. | ▪ Wash and dry greens. | ▪ Make Mushroom Tart filling. Garnish tart.<br><br>**BEFORE SERVING:**<br>▪ Toss salad.<br>▪ Warm soup. Garnish.<br>▪ Bake muffins.<br>▪ Bake strata. |
| ▪ Clean house. Iron tablecloths & napkins.<br>▪ Confirm arrangements with outside help.<br>▪ Set-up buffet & seating areas. | ▪ Chill sparkling wines, white wines, & beer.<br>▪ Set out dinner plates, tableware, & napkins.<br>▪ Prepare coffee maker. Set coffee/tea service on tray.<br>▪ Do final cleaning of kitchen & bathroom. | ▪ Shower, dress, & prepare for the party!<br>▪ Feed young children.<br>▪ Move pets to safe place.<br>▪ Pour juice into pitcher.<br>▪ Pour creamer into pitcher.<br>▪ Light candles.<br>▪ Put on music.<br>▪ Arrange food & drinks on buffet or table. |

# *Sweet Potato Muffins*

*Invest in a good trigger-release ice cream scoop for portioning muffin batter, cookie dough, and ice cream, of course! Muffins and cookies will all be the same size and cook evenly. Also, this method is way less messy.*

1 sweet potato, about ½ pound (225 g)

1 tablespoon unsalted butter, for greasing

1½ cups (220 g) flour

¾ teaspoon salt

2 teaspoons baking powder

1 teaspoon baking soda

1 teaspoon ground allspice

⅛ teaspoon ground cloves

½ teaspoon ground cinnamon

½ teaspoon ground ginger

¾ stick (6 tablespoons/85 g) unsalted butter, softened

⅔ cup (50 g) packed brown sugar

2 eggs, lightly beaten

½ cup (120 ml) milk

¾ cup (175 ml) pure maple syrup

*makes twelve muffins*

**EARLY PREPARATION:**

- Boil sweet potato and purée as directed below.

**PROCEDURE:**

For sweet potato, cover sweet potato with cold water and bring to a boil; reduce heat and simmer until tender when pierced with a knife, about 30 minutes. Drain and allow to cool slightly; peel and cut into several pieces. Purée sweet potato in food processor until smooth. (You should have about ¾ cup purée.) Set aside.

Preheat oven to 350°F (180°C). Generously grease a 12 cup muffin tin with butter or line with paper baking cups.

Sift together flour, salt, baking powder, baking soda, allspice, cloves, cinnamon, and ginger in a large bowl.

Beat butter and brown sugar with an electric mixer until creamy, about 1 minute on medium speed and 3 minutes on high. Add eggs and mix until well blended. Then beat in milk, maple syrup, and reserved sweet potato purée. Mix thoroughly.

Make a well in center of the dry ingredients and pour the liquid mixture into the well. Stir until ingredients are incorporated. Do not overmix.

Fill muffin cups three-quarters full with batter and bake for about 25 minutes or until a wooden pick inserted in center comes out clean. Transfer to a wire rack to cool before serving.

**CHEFS' TIP:**

*The muffin recipe is delicious with either yam or sweet potato.*

# *Maple Butter*

*You can also use this method of flavoring butter to create tasty spreads for other breads. Chive and garlic make a great combination for use on a baguette. Cumin and honey would be wonderful for cornbread. The same technique could be used to flavor cream cheese.*

1 stick (½ cup/115 g) unsalted butter, room temperature

2 tablespoons pure maple syrup

1 teaspoon finely minced lemon zest

Pinch salt

*for twelve muffins*

**PROCEDURE:**

Beat butter in food processor or mixer until creamy and fluffy. Scrape down sides of bowl and continue mixing until you have a uniform consistency without lumps. Add maple syrup, lemon zest, and salt. Blend well. Transfer maple butter into a small ceramic bowl and smooth the surface. Keep at room temperature if using within 2 hours, or chill and bring back to room temperature before serving.

**CHEFS' TIP:**

*We like to pipe the maple butter onto a cookie sheet lined with parchment paper to make little serving size rosettes. Place the cookie sheet in the freezer until the rosettes are solid and then transfer them to a small resealable plastic bag. Store in the freezer until the day before the event.*

# *Apple-Butternut Squash Soup*

*Sherry adds a nice nutty flavor to many soups and sauces. I like to add a splash at the end for maximum flavor.*

**SOUP**

1 butternut squash, about 2 pounds (900 g)

3 tablespoons olive oil, divided

3 Granny Smith apples

1 medium yellow onion, chopped

2 tablespoons dry sherry

½ teaspoon kosher or sea salt

⅛ teaspoon white pepper

4 cups (850 ml) chicken broth

1½ cups (360 ml) apple juice

1 cup (240 ml) heavy cream

1 teaspoon chopped fresh thyme

**GARNISH**

½ cup (50 g) slivered almonds, lightly toasted

¼ cup (15 g) cut fresh chives, about 1-inch (2.5 cm) long pieces

**CHEFS' TIP:**

*Most soups are better if "aged" for a couple of days. I like to make them ahead of time and let the flavors meld. Serve the soup in pottery for a casual gathering, or in tea cups for a ladies' day.*

*serves eight*

**EARLY PREPARATION:**

- Bake and purée squash as directed below.
- Toast almonds in 350°F (180°C) oven, about 7 to 8 minutes, until lightly browned.
- Cut chives into 1-inch (2.5 cm) pieces.

**PROCEDURE:**

For squash, preheat oven to 400°F (200°C). Cut squash in half lengthwise, scoop out seeds and place flesh-side down on cookie sheet that has been brushed with 1 tablespoon olive oil. Bake until soft and skin is easily pierced with a knife, about 40 minutes. When cool enough to handle, scoop out flesh and reserve. Throw away skins.

Peel apples and slice in rough 1-inch (2.5 cm) pieces, removing seeds.

Heat remaining 2 tablespoons olive oil in a large heavy-bottomed pot and add onions. Cook over medium-low heat, stirring occasionally until onions are translucent, about 5 minutes. Add apple pieces and cook for another 5 minutes, stirring occasionally. Stir in squash, 1 tablespoon sherry, salt, and white pepper. Pour in chicken broth and apple juice and bring to a simmer. Simmer 10 minutes and add heavy cream, thyme, and remaining 1 tablespoon sherry. Bring back to a simmer and remove from heat. Soup can be mashed with a potato masher for a chunkier texture or puréed in a blender for a smooth texture. Taste and season with additional salt and pepper if necessary.

Hold warm if serving within 1 hour or chill for reheating later. Reheat on stove over low heat.

Serve garnished with toasted almonds and chives.

# *Roasted Poblano Chile and Sausage Strata*

*Canned chiles may be substituted for the fresh poblanos, but it is really worth the extra effort to roast them yourself.*

2 poblano chiles, about ¼ pound (115 g) total

¾ pound (340 g) mild Italian sausage

1 tablespoon butter, for greasing

¼ cup (40 g) flour

¾ teaspoon kosher or sea salt

½ teaspoon baking powder

6 eggs

2 tablespoons unsalted butter, melted

1 cup (225 g) ricotta cheese

8 ounces (225 g) sharp white cheddar cheese, grated

*serves eight*

**EARLY PREPARATION:**

- Prepare chiles as directed below.
- Cook sausage as directed below.
- Grate cheese.

**PROCEDURE:**

For chiles, preheat broiler and place chiles directly on oven rack about 2 inches (5 cm) from broiler element. Rotate chiles when skins are black and blistered, about 5 minutes per side. When entire chile is blistered, transfer to a bowl and cover tightly. When chiles are cool enough to handle, peel, seed, and dice into ¼-inch (5 mm) pieces and set aside.

For sausage, cook and stir sausage in a skillet over medium heat until cooked through. Drain off excess fat and set aside.

Preheat oven to 350°F (180°C). Grease a 2 quart (2 l) casserole dish with butter.

Sift together flour, salt, and baking powder in a small bowl. Beat eggs in a large bowl with an electric mixer until eggs double in volume, about 3 minutes. Add butter, flour mixture, ricotta cheese, and cheddar cheese. Blend well.

Stir in chilies and sausage. Pour into casserole dish and bake in oven for 35 to 40 minutes or until the top is brown and puffed and a tester comes out clean.

Serve immediately.

# *Mushroom Tart*

*If you have trouble rolling out pie dough, as I do, try rolling the dough just slightly and then pressing it into the pan with your hands, making it as smooth as possible.*

**PASTRY SHELL**

2½ cups (400 g) flour

1½ teaspoons salt

2 sticks (1 cup/225 g) unsalted butter, room temperature

1 egg yolk

**MUSHROOM FILLING**

1 tablespoon olive oil

2 pounds (900 g) mushrooms, thinly sliced

2 tablespoons dry sherry

1½ cups (350 ml) heavy cream

½ teaspoon kosher or sea salt

¼ teaspoon freshly ground black pepper

8 green onions, sliced ¼-inch (5 mm) thick

2 tablespoons chopped fresh tarragon

Kosher or sea salt to taste

White pepper to taste

12 cherry tomatoes, halved

*serves eight*

**EARLY PREPARATION:**

- Slice mushrooms with knife or wire slicer. Refrigerate.

**PROCEDURE:**

**PASTRY SHELL**

Sift flour and salt into a large bowl. Cut butter into flour by hand with a pastry blender or using a food processor until it resembles coarse meal. Add egg yolk and mix by hand or processor until dough forms a ball. Work dough to hold it together. Refrigerate for 1 hour.

Preheat oven to 350°F (180°C).

Roll out dough into a round about ¼-inch (5 mm) thick and place in a 10 inch (25.5 cm) removable-bottomed tart pan. Remove excess dough from edge leaving a clean finish.

Bake 12 to 15 minutes until light brown. Cool slightly and remove from pan.

**MUSHROOM FILLING**

Heat olive oil in a large skillet over medium heat. Add mushrooms. Cook and stir mushrooms for about 1 minute. Add sherry and cook for another 2 minutes. Stir in heavy cream. Add salt and pepper. Simmer over medium heat, stirring occasionally, until cream has reduced by half and mixture has thickened considerably, about 25 to 30 minutes. Add green onions and fresh tarragon and cook for about 1 more minute. Season to taste with salt and white pepper. Cool slightly. Pour into pre-baked pastry shell. Garnish with cherry tomatoes around the edge and serve slightly warm.

# *Fresh Greens with Shallot-Lemon Vinaigrette*

*I really like the fresh, zippy flavor of this dressing. For a light dressing it is packed with flavor and enhances the greens rather than drowning them. I love to use arugula, but you may want to use your own favorite salad green.*

**VINAIGRETTE**

1 tablespoon minced shallots

2 tablespoons sherry vinegar

1 teaspoon minced lemon zest

1 teaspoon fresh lemon juice

¼ cup (60 ml) extra virgin olive oil

2 tablespoons minced chives

⅛ teaspoon kosher or sea salt

⅛ teaspoon black pepper

⅛ teaspoon sugar

**GREENS**

1 pound (450 g) arugula (rocket) or other fresh greens, torn into bite-size pieces

*serves eight*

**EARLY PREPARATION:**

- Remove zest from lemon; then juice.
- Mince chives, store in plastic bag.
- Wash and dry greens.

**PROCEDURE:**

**VINAIGRETTE**

Mix all dressing ingredients together.

**GREENS**

Place salad greens in a plastic bag or a bowl covered with plastic wrap; refrigerate until ready to serve.

Toss salad greens with vinaigrette immediately before serving.

# *Fall/Winter Brunch* shopping list

*This is a complete list of ingredients you will need to make all the recipes in this menu, along with the quantity you will need for each ingredient. The menus are designed to feed a gathering of eight. If increasing or decreasing any recipes be certain to adjust quantities on the shopping list. Check your pantry before shopping, as you may already have enough of many of these items.*

### PRODUCE

- ☐ Apples, Granny Smith (3)
- ☐ Butternut squash (1 about 2 lbs./900 g)
- ☐ Cherry tomatoes (12)
- ☐ Green onions (8)
- ☐ Greens, mixed, or arugula (1 lb./450 g)
- ☐ Lemon (1)
- ☐ Mushrooms (2 lbs./900 g)
- ☐ Onion, yellow (1 medium)
- ☐ Poblano chiles (2 about ¼ lb./115 g)
- ☐ Shallots (1)
- ☐ Sweet potato (1 about ½ lb./225 g)

### HERBS

- ☐ Chives, fresh (½ cup/25 g)
- ☐ Tarragon, fresh (2 Tbs.)
- ☐ Thyme, fresh (1 tsp.)

### DAIRY/EGGS

- ☐ Butter, unsalted (1 lb./450 g)
- ☐ Cheddar cheese, sharp white (8 oz./225 g)
- ☐ Heavy cream (20 oz./600 ml)
- ☐ Milk (4 oz./120 ml)
- ☐ Ricotta cheese (8 oz./225 g)
- ☐ Eggs, large (9)

### MEAT

- ☐ Mild Italian sausage ( ¾ lb./340 g)

### BAKING GOODS/SPICES

- ☐ Allspice, ground (1 tsp.)
- ☐ Cinnamon, ground (½ tsp.)
- ☐ Cloves, ground (⅛ tsp.)
- ☐ Ginger, ground (½ tsp.)
- ☐ Pure maple syrup (8 oz./240 ml)
- ☐ Slivered almonds (2 oz./50 g)

### CANNED GOODS

- ☐ Chicken broth (32 oz./850 ml)

### CONDIMENTS

- ☐ Sherry vinegar (2 Tbs.)

### PANTRY STAPLES

- ☐ Baking powder (2½ tsp.)
- ☐ Baking soda (1 tsp.)
- ☐ Flour, all-purpose (4¼ cups/660 g)
- ☐ Olive oil, extra virgin (½ cup/120 ml)
- ☐ Salt, kosher or sea
- ☐ Sugar, brown (⅔ cup/50 g)
- ☐ Pepper, black
- ☐ Pepper, white

### SUPPLIES

- ☐ Paper baking cups (12)
- ☐ Tart pan with removable bottom

### BEVERAGES

- ☐ Apple juice (12 oz./360 ml)
- ☐ Coffee varietal (Sumatra)

### WINE

- ☐ Chardonnay
- ☐ Dry sherry (4 Tbs.)
- ☐ Sparkling wines

# *fall/winter buffet*

*a*mong the advantages of a buffet party is that you can enjoy your guests' company while they fill their plates at leisure. All of your hard work comes to easy fruition once the dishes are set out, and you don't have to worry about setting a big table and refilling plates. There is often an abundance of formal meals in the fall and winter seasons, and an informal but gourmet buffet will be a welcome change.

This menu caters to a variety of tastes and ensures that everyone finds something to love. The Oven-Roasted Vegetable and Mozzarella Napoleons make a beautiful presentation. The marinade for the chicken kebabs produces a flavorful, tender, and moist chicken. Adding to this buffet is Potato and Watercress Salad, which boasts a wonderful Lemon Vinaigrette. It's a light change from the standard cloying mayonnaise dressing.

When setting up the buffet table, the flatware and napkins are best placed at the end. Remember to put the drinks at a separate table to encourage mingling.

Cumin-Garlic Chicken Kebabs deserve to be served with a Sauvignon Blanc. Fennel-Crusted Tuna goes well with a Merlot. Add a good quality porter beer to the table, and finish with an Italian Roast Espresso to round out the beverage selection.

FALL/WINTER

# *Buffet Menu*

*Fall Greens with Walnuts and Gorgonzola with Apple Cider Vinaigrette*

PAGE 28

*Fennel-Crusted Tuna*

PAGE 29

*Cumin-Garlic Chicken Kebabs*

PAGE 30

*Oven-Roasted Vegetable and Mozzarella Napoleons*

PAGE 31

*Potato and Watercress Salad with Lemon Vinaigrette*

PAGE 32

*Warm herb rolls*
(Purchase fresh from bakery)

BEVERAGE SUGGESTIONS

*Sauvignon Blanc*

*Merlot*

*Porter Beer*

*Italian Roast Espresso*

*Photo: Fennel-Crusted Tuna*

FALL/WINTER

# Buffet *planning guide*

| | **ADVANCE PREPARATIONS** | **PREP TIME** *(2 to 3 Days Ahead)* |
|---|---|---|
| Hospitality  | ▪ Create guest list. Call or send out invitations.<br>▪ Provide directions if needed. | ▪ Call any guests who have not responded.<br>▪ Talk to neighbors & plan parking arrangements. |
| Shopping  | ▪ Print shopping list & menu from www.seahillpress.com website.<br>▪ Review shopping list & check your staples. | ▪ Purchase beverages & non-perishable groceries (not tuna or rolls). |
| 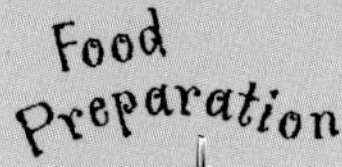 Food Preparation  | ▪ Clean & organize refrigerator. | ▪ Make vinaigrette for Fall Greens. Refrigerate.<br>▪ Toast walnuts for greens & store at room temperature.<br>▪ Crumble Gorgonzola & wrap well. Refrigerate.<br>▪ Make fennel crust mixture for Fennel-Crusted Tuna.<br>▪ Prepare chicken marinade. |
| Staging  | ▪ Sketch a diagram of seating plan, table set-up, & placement of items. Plan seating arrangements.<br>▪ Plan & purchase tableware and decorations.<br>▪ Borrow or purchase needed cookware & serving dishes.<br>▪ Schedule housecleaner or childcare if needed.<br>▪ Ask friends or family for specific help if needed.<br>▪ Decide what to wear. | ▪ Gather, wash, & polish serving platters, utensils, dishes, & glassware.<br>▪ Cover all items with plastic wrap or tablecloth to keep clean.<br>▪ Organize serving areas. Borrow buffet or card tables if needed. |

*Preparation for this menu spreads itself out evenly over the week before the event, leaving you more time on the big day. Purchase the tuna the day before or with the rolls the day of your party for the freshest taste. These are just guidelines to help your party go as smoothly as possible. Remember that you are not bound to follow these precisely. Have fun!*

| DAY BEFORE EVENT | DAY OF EVENT | LAST TWO HOURS |
|---|---|---|
| | ▪ Assist guests with last-minute questions & requests. | |
| | ▪ Purchase last-minute items such as tuna, rolls, ice, & flowers. | |
| ▪ Cut chicken & add to marinade. Refrigerate.<br>▪ Prepare Lemon Vinaigrette for potato salad.<br>▪ Wash & pick watercress leaves for potato salad.<br>▪ Cut chives for Potato & Watercress Salad. Refrigerate. | ▪ Wash & dry Fall Greens.<br>▪ Assemble Oven-Roasted Vegetable Napoleons.<br>▪ Finish Potato & Watercress Salad.<br>▪ Soak wooden skewers. | **BEFORE SERVING:**<br>▪ Cook chicken.<br>▪ Crust tuna & cook.<br>▪ Heat Napoleons.<br>▪ Dice apple for Fall Greens & toss salad with dressing.<br>▪ Warm rolls in oven. |
| ▪ Set up serving tables with pedestals, tablecloths, & decorations.<br>▪ Clean house. Iron tablecloths & napkins.<br>▪ Set out flatware, napkins, & dinner plates.<br>▪ Confirm arrangements with outside help.<br>▪ Set-up buffet and seating areas. | ▪ Chill white wines & beer.<br>▪ Prepare coffee maker. Set coffee/tea service on tray.<br>▪ Do final cleaning of kitchen & bathroom. | ▪ Try to relax - take a 20 minute siesta or do some leisurely reading.<br>▪ Shower, dress, & prepare yourself for the party!<br>▪ Move pets to safe places.<br>▪ Feed young children.<br>▪ Open red wine.<br>▪ Pour water into pitcher.<br>▪ Light candles.<br>▪ Put on music.<br>▪ Pour cream into pitcher.<br>▪ Arrange food & drinks on buffet or table. |

# *Fall Greens with Walnuts and Gorgonzola with Apple Cider Vinaigrette*

*Reduced apple cider adds a wonderful sweetness to this dressing, mellowing the bite of the intense cider vinegar.*

**APPLE CIDER VINAIGRETTE**

1 cup (240 ml) apple cider

¼ cup (60 ml) apple cider vinegar

2 teaspoons brown sugar

1 teaspoon Dijon mustard

⅛ teaspoon kosher or sea salt

⅛ teaspoon freshly ground black pepper

⅔ cup (160 ml) vegetable oil

**MIXED GREENS SALAD**

1 pound (450 g) mixed fall greens: frisée, mâche, Bibb (butter) lettuce (Can use a seasonal mix sold by the pound in most grocery stores.)

1 apple (Red Delicious, Braeburn, or your own personal favorite)

½ cup (50 g) walnuts, lightly toasted

⅓ cup (75 g) crumbled Gorgonzola cheese

1 recipe Apple Cider Vinaigrette

*serves eight*

**EARLY PREPARATION:**

- Make vinaigrette.
- Toast walnuts in preheated oven (350°F/180°C) for about 6 to 8 minutes.
- Crumble Gorgonzola and refrigerate.
- Wash greens and dry between paper towels.

**PROCEDURE:**

**APPLE CIDER VINAIGRETTE**

Heat apple cider in a small saucepan and simmer over medium heat until reduced to approximately ¼ cup (60 ml), about 15 minutes. Cool. Blend all vinaigrette ingredients together.

**MIXED GREENS SALAD**

Place washed greens in a large salad bowl. Dice apple into ¼-inch (5 mm) small pieces, leaving peel on. Toss walnuts, greens, apples, and Gorgonzola with vinaigrette immediately before serving.

**CHEFS' TIP:**

*You may not need all of the vinaigrette on the salad. Toss the salad with some vinaigrette and leave the rest in a decorative container so that guests may add more if they desire.*

# *Fennel-Crusted Tuna*

*Don't let the short list of ingredients and simplicity of this recipe deceive you. The texture and taste of the fennel crust with the meaty fresh tuna is sensational! I strongly recommend that you cook the tuna rare to medium-rare.*

2 pounds (900 g) fresh tuna, skinned, trimmed, and cut into 2-inch (5 cm) thick pieces

3 tablespoons fennel seed

¾ teaspoon kosher or sea salt

1½ teaspoons ground coriander

1½ teaspoons ground white pepper

2 egg whites

3 tablespoons olive oil

**CHEFS' TIP:**

*How adventurous your guests are may determine how you choose to cook the tuna. We highly recommend buying a good quality tuna (ahi or yellowtail sashimi grade) and cooking it rare to medium-rare. Beyond medium-rare the meat gets dry and almost mealy. Serve the tuna with a smattering of wasabi, spicy Japanese horseradish, if you'd like. Wasabi is available in the Asian section of the grocery store in powder form or as a paste.*

*serves eight*

**EARLY PREPARATION:**

- Prepare fennel crust mixture as described below.

**PROCEDURE:**

For fennel crust, grind fennel seed and salt in a coffee grinder. Mix with coriander and white pepper. Put spice mixture into a pie tin or other flat, low-sided dish.

Whip egg whites in another pie tin or dish, until they are just broken up.

Dip tuna pieces into egg white and then into spice mixture.

Heat olive oil in a heavy-bottomed sauté pan and sear tuna on both sides, about 1 to 2 minutes per side.

Tuna can be served hot, room temperature, or chilled. Slice on the diagonal into about ½-inch (1 cm) slices and serve.

# *Cumin-Garlic Chicken Kebabs*

*Moist, moist, moist! The marinade on this chicken makes it almost impossible to overcook!*

**MARINADE**

3 tablespoons cumin seed

⅓ cup (80 ml) vegetable oil

4 garlic cloves, minced

3 tablespoons Dijon mustard

3 tablespoons honey

½ teaspoon kosher or sea salt

¼ teaspoon freshly ground black pepper

**KEBABS**

2 pounds (900 g) boneless, skinless chicken breasts, cut into 1½-inch (4 cm) cubes

16 small wooden skewers, soaked in water for 30 minutes

*serves eight*

**EARLY PREPARATION:**

- Prepare marinade.
- Soak skewers in water.

**PROCEDURE:**

**MARINADE**

Cook and stir cumin seed in a small, dry skillet over medium heat, until toasted and fragrant, about 2 minutes. Set aside to cool. Grind cumin seed in a coffee grinder or mini processor. Transfer cumin to a bowl and stir in oil, garlic, mustard, honey, salt, and pepper. Store mixture in a container suitable for marinating.

**KEBABS**

Add chicken to marinade and refrigerate 24 hours.

Preheat broiler or light barbecue grill.

Thread chicken onto skewers using 2 to 3 pieces per skewer. Bake on a cookie sheet under broiler, or cook on barbecue grill, turning after 3 to 4 minutes per side, until cooked through. Serve hot.

# *Oven-Roasted Vegetable and Mozzarella Napoleons*

*These simple do-ahead vegetables are showstoppers! I use fresh mozzarella which has a mellow flavor and a soft texture. You can use regular mozzarella. It melts quite a bit while warming, but still tastes great!*

1 large Italian eggplant (aubergine), cut into ¼-inch (5 mm) rounds

2 medium zucchini, cut into ¼-inch (5 mm) bias rounds

2 yellow bell peppers, each cut lengthwise into 4 pieces

8 mushrooms

4 tablespoons olive oil

¾ teaspoon kosher or sea salt

½ teaspoon freshly ground black pepper

2 (2 ounces/55 g) fresh mozzarella balls, sliced into ¼-inch (5 mm) rounds

3 Roma tomatoes, cored and cut lengthwise into ¼-inch (5 mm) slices

Fresh rosemary sprigs, for skewering (optional)

⅔ cup (150 ml) chicken broth

*serves eight*

**PROCEDURE:**

Preheat broiler. Brush eggplant, zucchini, yellow peppers, and mushrooms lightly with olive oil on both sides. Season with salt and black pepper.

Quickly broil vegetables on a cookie sheet, 2 inches below broiler (about 3 minutes per side) making sure not to thoroughly cook them. Transfer them to another cookie sheet and spread them out to cool. When cool, layer vegetables on top of one another starting with the eggplant on the bottom followed by mozzarella, zucchini, tomatoes, yellow peppers, and mushrooms. Optional: You may secure the stack by skewering through the middle with a rosemary sprig.

Place "Napoleons" on a cookie sheet or in a casserole dish and refrigerate until ready to bake.

For heating, preheat oven to 375°F (190°C). Warm chicken broth and pour around Napoleons. If using rosemary skewers, wrap a piece of lettuce around the top, leafy part of rosemary and cover lettuce with a small piece of foil. This will keep the herb from charring and will make for a beautiful presentation. Bake for 10 to 12 minutes or until just heated through. Serve immediately.

# *Potato and Watercress Salad with Lemon Vinaigrette*

*Watercress is available year round. It has a slightly peppery flavor. You may substitute spinach or any other mild leafy green if you can't find it.*

**LEMON VINAIGRETTE**

¼ cup (60 ml) fresh lemon juice (about 2 lemons)

1 teaspoon garlic, minced

1 teaspoon Dijon mustard

1 teaspoon sugar

⅔ cup (160 ml) vegetable oil

⅛ teaspoon kosher or sea salt

⅛ teaspoon white pepper

**POTATO AND WATERCRESS SALAD**

2 pounds (900 g) medium new red potatoes, halved

1 recipe Lemon Vinaigrette

2 bunches (½ pound/225 g) watercress, washed and tough stems removed

10 radishes, cut into ¼-inch (5 mm) pieces

½ cup (25 g) chives, bias cut into 1-inch (2.5 cm) pieces

Kosher or sea salt to taste

Freshly ground black pepper

*serves eight*

**EARLY PREPARATION:**

- Prepare lemon vinaigrette.
- Wash and pick watercress.
- Cut chives.

**PROCEDURE:**

**LEMON VINAIGRETTE**

Place lemon juice, garlic, mustard, and sugar into small food processor or blender. While machine is running, slowly drizzle in oil. Season with salt and white pepper.

**POTATO AND WATERCRESS SALAD**

Place potatoes in a saucepan and cover with cold water; add salt. Bring to a simmer and cook until slightly tender but still firm, about 10 minutes once simmering. Carefully drain the potatoes and while still hot put them into a bowl and toss with half of the vinaigrette.

Toss potatoes, watercress, radishes, chives, and remaining vinaigrette together. Season with salt and black pepper. Serve immediately while still slightly warm or refrigerate and pull out to room temperature for later use.

**CHEFS' TIP:**

*There are a great number of substitutions available for watercress if you can't find it, don't like it or just prefer something else: spinach, arugula, frisée or any other leafy green that adds a splash of color and a little crunch will work well.*

# *Fall/Winter Buffet* *shopping list*

*This is a complete list of ingredients you will need to make all the recipes in this menu, along with the quantity you will need for each ingredient. The menus are designed to feed a gathering of eight. If increasing or decreasing any recipes be certain to adjust quantities on the shopping list. Check your pantry before shopping, as you may already have enough of many of these items.*

### PRODUCE

- ☐ Apple: Red Delicious, Braeburn, or your own personal favorite (1)
- ☐ Eggplant, Italian (aubergine) (1 large)
- ☐ Garlic (1 head)
- ☐ Greens, mixed fall: frisée, mâche, Bibb (butter) lettuce (1 lb./450 g)
- ☐ Lemons (3)
- ☐ Mushrooms (8)
- ☐ Peppers, yellow bell (2)
- ☐ Potatoes, medium new red (2 lbs./900 g)
- ☐ Radishes (10)
- ☐ Tomatoes, Roma (3)
- ☐ Watercress (2 bunches/225 g)
- ☐ Zucchini (2 medium)

### HERBS

- ☐ Chives, fresh (½ cup/25 g)
- ☐ Rosemary sprigs, fresh (8)

### DAIRY/EGGS

- ☐ Gorgonzola cheese (⅓ cup/75 g)
- ☐ Mozzarella cheese, fresh (2 x 2 oz./55 g)
- ☐ Eggs, large (2)

### POULTRY/FISH

- ☐ Chicken breasts, boneless, skinless (2 pounds/900 g)
- ☐ Tuna, fresh (2 pounds/900 g)

### BAKERY

- ☐ Herb rolls

### BAKING GOODS/SPICES

- ☐ Coriander, ground (1½ tsp.)
- ☐ Cumin seed (3 Tbs.)
- ☐ Fennel seed (3 Tbs.)
- ☐ Walnuts (½ cup/50 g)

### CANNED GOODS

- ☐ Chicken broth (⅔ cup/160 ml)

### CONDIMENTS

- ☐ Apple cider vinegar (¼ cup/60 ml)
- ☐ Dijon mustard (4 Tbs.)
- ☐ Honey (3 Tbs.)

### PANTRY STAPLES

- ☐ Oil, olive (7 Tbs.)
- ☐ Oil, vegetable (1⅔ cups/400 ml)
- ☐ Pepper, fresh black
- ☐ Pepper, ground white
- ☐ Salt, kosher or sea
- ☐ Sugar, brown (2 tsp.)
- ☐ Sugar, white (2 tsp.)

### BEVERAGES

- ☐ Apple cider (1 cup/240 ml)
- ☐ Beer, porter
- ☐ Espresso, Italian Roast
- ☐ Merlot
- ☐ Sauvignon Blanc

### SUPPLIES

- ☐ 16 small wooden skewers

# *fall/winter picnic*

*A* picnic in winter? Absolutely! Think of a hearty meal served at a tailgate party outside your home team's stadium, or a break at a lodge from a long day of fresh powder skiing with your friends. A hike through the woods followed by a picnic would offer a wonderful way to enjoy the display of fall foliage with your good friends. There are an abundance of reasons to eat outside during the fall or winter, and this menu gives you one more excuse.

These dishes can be prepared ahead of time and transported easily. Hearty soup eaten outside on a brisk day is the ultimate luxury, and the Winter Seafood Chowder is a far cry from chili. Transport the soup in a large thermal container to keep it warm. White Bean and Roasted Garlic Salad is rich, satisfying, and full of flavor.

If this is a sports event, decorate with the theme! Use the team colors, and a football helmet full of flowers. Or, if you're pausing during a ski day, create a few large paper snowflakes to decorate your serving area. Bring along a bunch of tied flowers, a pretty potted plant, or a basket of pinecones for decoration. Bring an umbrella and a stand along to cover food in case of foul weather. Use a covered lantern instead of candles to highlight the food.

For this menu, you could serve some slightly unusual drinks, such as a Johannisberg Riesling. And, as odd as it may sound for the cold, a good hearty porter or stout beer would be wonderfully warming.

FALL/WINTER

# *Picnic Menu*

*Winter Seafood Chowder*

PAGE 40

*Pecorino and Pepperoncini Wraps*

PAGE 41

*White Bean and Roasted Garlic Salad*

PAGE 42

*Individual herb rolls or crunchy French baguette*

*(From bakery)*

*Almond Cookies*

PAGE 43

BEVERAGE SUGGESTIONS

*Johannisberg Riesling*

*Porter or Stout Beer*

*Merlot*

*Photo: Winter Seafood Chowder*

# Picnic *planning guide*

| | ADVANCE PREPARATIONS | PREP TIME *(2 to 3 Days Ahead)* |
|---|---|---|
| Hospitality | ▪ Reserve picnic site.<br>▪ Create guest list. Call or send invitations.<br>▪ Provide directions if needed.<br>▪ Print shopping list & menu from www.seahillpress.com website. | ▪ Call any guests who have not responded.<br>▪ Confirm your meeting spot & parking plans. |
| Shopping  | ▪ Locate & purchase hearts of palm.<br>▪ Purchase ingredients for Almond Cookies. | ▪ Purchase beverages & all non-perishable groceries (not seafood). |
| Food Preparation  | ▪ Make Almond Cookies up to one week in advance. Freeze. | ▪ Roast garlic for White Bean Salad & store at room temperature. |
| Staging  | ▪ Clean & organize refrigerator.<br>▪ Plan & purchase tableware & decorations.<br>▪ Borrow or purchase needed cookware, serving dishes, portable seating & tables, & portable stereo.<br>▪ Schedule help or childcare if needed.<br>▪ Decide what to wear. | ▪ Gather serving platters, utensils, dishes, & glassware.<br>▪ Gather & wash containers for transporting food. |

*This menu is marvelous for doing ahead so you can get out quickly on the day of your picnic. These are just guidelines to help your party go as smoothly as possible. Remember that you are not bound to follow these precisely. Have fun!*

| DAY BEFORE EVENT | DAY OF EVENT | LAST TWO HOURS |
|---|---|---|
| | ▪ Assist guests with last-minute questions & requests. | |
| ▪ Purchase halibut, prawns, & scallops. | ▪ Go to store for last-minute items: bread for soup. | |
| ▪ Make Seafood Chowder.<br>▪ Make Pecorino & Pepperoncini Wraps. Assemble on serving plate & refrigerate.<br>▪ Make White Bean Salad. Refrigerate in serving bowl.<br>▪ Transfer Almond Cookies from freezer to refrigerator. | | ▪ Warm Seafood Chowder & pour into thermal container. |
| ▪ Chill white wines & beer.<br>▪ Confirm arrangements with outside help.<br>▪ Pack serving dishes & utensils, tableware, cups, portable seating & tables, & portable stereo & music. | ▪ Check that all plates, flatware, napkins, cups, & utensils are ready. | ▪ At Picnic Site: Open red wine. |

# *Winter Seafood Chowder*

2 tablespoons olive oil

1 large yellow onion, diced

2 cloves garlic, minced

6 new red potatoes, diced

2 large leeks, cleaned and sliced, ¼-inch (5 mm) thick slices

2 tablespoons chopped celery leaf (optional)

4 Roma tomatoes, diced

2 tablespoons Chardonnay

4 cups (1 l) chicken broth or fish stock

Pinch red pepper flakes

1 teaspoon chopped fresh marjoram

Pinch orange zest

Hot pepper sauce to taste

2 tablespoons olive oil

1 tablespoon butter

½ pound (225 g) halibut, cut into ½-inch (1 cm) chunks

12 sea scallops

12 prawns, (21-25 count) shelled and deveined

*serves eight*

**PROCEDURE:**

Heat olive oil in an 8 to 10 quart stockpot. Add onion, garlic, potatoes, leeks, and celery leaf and cook over medium-high heat until wilted, about 5 minutes. Add tomatoes, and stir until they begin to melt down, about 5 minutes. Add wine, chicken broth or fish stock, red pepper flakes, marjoram, orange zest, hot pepper sauce, and olive oil. Bring to a simmer. Simmer for 20 minutes, until potatoes begin to fall apart.

Heat butter in a skillet. Add halibut, scallops, and prawns and quickly sauté over medium-high heat just until prawns turn color, about 3 to 5 minutes. Remove from heat. Once soup stock starts to thicken, add seafood and stir.

Refrigerate chowder until ready to reheat and serve. To reheat, warm gently in stockpot on low heat.

**CHEFS' TIP:**

*Save shrimp shells and freeze to make a flavorful stock later. Just cover with water and simmer 25 to 30 minutes; strain.*

# *Pecorino and Pepperoncini Wraps*

½ pound (225 g) soft pecorino or other soft farmer's cheese

12 pepperoncini

*serves eight as an appetizer*

**PROCEDURE:**

Cut cheese into 1½-inch (4 cm) long strips or logs. Slice pepperoncini in half lengthwise. Roll up cheese strips in pepperoncini slices and secure with wooden picks.

# *White Bean and Roasted Garlic Salad*

*Begin this wonderful salad a day ahead of time, as the flavor is enhanced when the ingredients have been left to mingle for 12 to 24 hours before serving. This versatile side dish can also be a main dish for another occasion, just add some lettuce and poached chicken or fish.*

2 heads garlic

1 tablespoon olive oil

2 (15 ounce/425 g) cans white beans, drained and rinsed

1 (14 ounce/400 g) can hearts of palm, sliced into ½-inch (1 cm) thick pieces

¼ cup (50 g) fresh sage, cut into very thin ribbons

¼ cup (60 ml) lemons

⅓ cup (75 ml) extra virgin olive oil

½ teaspoon kosher or sea salt

¼ teaspoon ground white pepper

*serves eight*

**EARLY PREPARATION:**

- Roast garlic as described below and store tightly covered in refrigerator.

**PROCEDURE:**

To roast garlic, preheat oven to 375°F (190°C). Using clean hands, rub garlic heads lightly with 1 tablespoon of olive oil and wrap loosely in foil. Bake until garlic head gives a bit with a gentle squeeze, about 35 to 40 minutes. Cool garlic until comfortable to handle. Using a serrated knife, slice off the root end to expose the large ends of the garlic cloves. Using both hands squeeze from the sprout end toward the root to extract the cloves. They should easily slide out if the garlic has been cooked properly and is still slightly warm. Roasted garlic may be stored in the refrigerator in a sealed container for up to one week.

Twelve to twenty-four hours before serving, mix the garlic, beans, hearts of palm, sage, lemon juice, olive oil, salt, and pepper together in a large bowl.

**STORAGE AND SERVING:**

Refrigerate in the serving bowl, covered with plastic wrap. Remove salad from the refrigerator 1 hour before serving. Serve at room temperature.

# *Almond Cookies*

*Have fun substituting another nut or a mixture of nuts instead of the almonds. Pistachios make fabulous cookies. Is there someone on your guest list who can't eat nuts? Just remember to bring along some nut-free cookies, and your guest will be honored by your thoughtfulness.*

1½ sticks (¾ cup/175 g) unsalted butter, plus extra for cookie sheet

½ cup (80 g) powdered sugar

1 cup (100 g) very finely chopped almonds

1½ cups (240 g) flour

1 teaspoon lemon extract or finely chopped lemon zest

½ teaspoon salt

*serves eight*

**PROCEDURE:**

Preheat oven to 350°F (180°C). Grease cookie sheet with butter.

Beat butter and sugar with an electric mixer until creamy. Sift the almonds through a coarse sieve to remove the larger pieces. Add almonds to butter mixture. Stir in flour, lemon extract or zest, and salt. Drop dough by tablespoons onto cookie sheet. Bake for 8 to 10 minutes, or until edges are just beginning to brown. Immediately remove from cookie sheet; cool.

**STORAGE:**

The cookies can be frozen for up to 1 month. Take them from the freezer and thaw at room temperature the night before the event.

# *Fall/Winter Picnic* *shopping list*

*This is a complete list of ingredients you will need to make all the recipes in this menu, along with the quantity you will need for each ingredient. The menus are designed to feed a gathering of eight. If increasing or decreasing any recipes be certain to adjust quantities on the shopping list. Check your pantry before shopping, as you may already have enough of many of these items.*

### PRODUCE

- ☐ Celery (2 Tbs.)
- ☐ Garlic (3 heads)
- ☐ Leeks, large (2)
- ☐ Lemons, for juice (2)
- ☐ Onion, large yellow (1)
- ☐ Orange (1)
- ☐ Potatoes, new red (6)
- ☐ Tomatoes, Roma (4)

### HERBS

- ☐ Marjoram, fresh (1 tsp.)
- ☐ Sage, fresh (¼ cup/50 g)

### DAIRY

- ☐ Butter, unsalted (1 cup/225 g)
- ☐ Pecorino, soft or other farmer's cheese (½ lb./225 g)

### FISH/SEAFOOD

- ☐ Halibut (½ lb./225 g)
- ☐ Prawns, 21-25 count
- ☐ Scallops, sea (12)

### BAKING GOODS/SPICES

- ☐ Almonds (1 cup/100 g)
- ☐ Lemon extract (1 tsp.)
- ☐ Red pepper flakes

### CANNED GOODS

- ☐ Chicken broth or fish stock (4 cups/1 l)
- ☐ Hearts of palm (14 oz./425 g)
- ☐ White beans (2 x 15 oz./425 g)

### CONDIMENTS

- ☐ Hot pepper sauce
- ☐ Pepperoncini (12)

### PANTRY STAPLES

- ☐ Flour, all-purpose (1½ cups/240 g)
- ☐ Olive oil, extra virgin (⅔ cup/150 ml)
- ☐ Pepper, ground white
- ☐ Salt, kosher or sea
- ☐ Sugar, powdered (½ cup/80 g)

### BAKERY

- ☐ Herb rolls or baguette

### BEVERAGES

- ☐ Beer, porter or stout
- ☐ Johannisberg Riesling
- ☐ Chardonnay (2 Tbs.)

### SUPPLIES

- ☐ Small wooden picks

# fall/winter hors d'oeuvres

hors d'oeuvres parties are fun to throw together at almost the last minute as an excuse to get together and sample an array of delicious food and wine. Call a couple of friends for an informal get-together anytime, because these recipes are fun and delicious enough to plan a night around. Or, make it a black-tie affair to celebrate one of the season's many holidays without planning a heavy sit-down meal. These recipes will be elegant enough for whatever you require. We think your guests will be pleased by the variety without the usual, tired meatball and cheese spread.

This interesting and delicious menu has a Mediterranean flair. The Creamy Blue and Mascarpone Tart is a savory taste sensation. It has a velvety rich yet surprisingly light texture. The sweet-sour Onion Marmalade is the perfect accompaniment. Broiled Oysters are a sophisticated offering. Roasted red beets resting on pale green endive leaves make a stunning presentation.

Stagger the presentation of each dish so that guests will have something new to try at different points in the party. The Sausage-Stuffed Mushrooms and Caramelized Pears and Prosciutto are great to have on a roving tray, periodically sent around the room. Try having at least two locations for serving the other dishes to encourage your guests to mingle.

Half the fun of an hors d'oeuvres party is sampling wines, so we recommend serving several. Have a mini-wine tasting along with your hors d'oeuvres by serving Riesling, Sauvignon Blanc, Chardonnay, Syrah, and Pinot Noir.

FALL/WINTER

# *Hors d'oeuvres Menu*

*Belgian Endive with Tarragon-Beet Relish*

PAGE 50

*Broiled Oysters with Shallot, Fennel, and Spinach Butter*

PAGE 51

*Sausage-Stuffed Mushrooms*

PAGE 52

*Cocktail Tortellini in Sun-Dried Tomato Basil Sauce*

PAGE 53

*Creamy Blue and Mascarpone Tart*

PAGE 54

*Onion Marmalade*

PAGE 55

*Caramelized Pears Wrapped in Prosciutto*

PAGE 56

BEVERAGE SUGGESTIONS

*Chardonnay, Riesling, Sauvignon Blanc, Syrah or Pinot Noir*

*Photo: Broiled Oysters with Shallot, Fennel, and Spinach Butter*

# Hors d'oeuvres *planning guide*

| | ADVANCE PREPARATIONS | PREP TIME *(2 to 3 Days Ahead)* |
|---|---|---|
| Hospitality  | ▪ Create guest list. Call or send invitations. Provide directions if needed.<br>▪ Print shopping list & menu from www.seahillpress.com website. | ▪ Call any guests who have not responded.<br>▪ Talk to neighbors & plan parking arrangements. |
| Shopping  | ▪ Review list of ingredients.<br>▪ Purchase ingredients for Shallot, Fennel, & Spinach Butter. | ▪ Purchase beverages & non-perishable groceries. |
| Food Preparation  | ▪ Clean & organize refrigerator.<br>▪ Make Shallot, Fennel, & Spinach Butter. Wrap tightly in plastic wrap. Freeze. | ▪ Roast beets, peel, dice & refrigerate.<br>▪ Make vinaigrette for beets.<br>▪ Prepare Sun-Dried Tomato Basil Sauce.<br>▪ Make Onion Marmalade. Refrigerate in airtight container. |
| Staging  | ▪ Sketch a diagram of table set-up & placement of items. Plan seating arrangements.<br>▪ Plan & purchase tableware & decorations.<br>▪ Borrow or purchase needed cookware & serving dishes.<br>▪ Select housecleaner or childcare if needed.<br>▪ Ask friends or family for specific help if needed.<br>▪ Decide what to wear. | ▪ Gather serving platters, utensils, dishes, & glassware.<br>▪ Cover items with plastic wrap or tablecloth to keep clean. |

*Hors d'oeuvres parties are perfect for wine tasting or cocktails. These are just guidelines to help your party go as smoothly as possible. Remember that you are not bound to follow these precisely. Have fun!*

| DAY BEFORE EVENT | DAY OF EVENT | LAST TWO HOURS |
|---|---|---|
| | ▪ Assist guests with last-minute questions & requests. | |
| ▪ Purchase oysters. | ▪ Purchase last-minute items: ice. | |
| ▪ Make Creamy Blue & Mascarpone Tart. Refrigerate.<br>▪ Toast almonds & prepare sausage stuffing. Refrigerate.<br>▪ Pull Shallot, Fennel, & Spinach Butter from freezer to refrigerator.<br>▪ Make Tarragon-Beet Relish. Refrigerate. | ▪ Stuff mushrooms & dot with butter. Refrigerate.<br>▪ Shuck oysters & leave on the half shell. Keep cold.<br>▪ Cook tortellini. | ▪ Drain liquid from beets.<br>▪ Bring tart & marmalade to room temperature.<br>**BEFORE SERVING:**<br>▪ Put relish on endive.<br>▪ Bake mushrooms.<br>▪ Place butter on oysters & broil.<br>▪ Combine tomato sauce with tortellini. Heat in dish.<br>▪ Make pears. |
| ▪ Clean house or party site. Iron tablecloths & napkins.<br>▪ Confirm arrangements with outside help.<br>▪ Set-up buffet & seating areas. | ▪ Chill white wines & beer.<br>▪ Set out tableware & plenty of cocktail napkins.<br>▪ Do final cleaning of kitchen & bathroom. | ▪ Try to relax - take a 20 minute siesta or do some leisurely reading.<br>▪ Shower, dress, & prepare yourself for the party!<br>▪ Move pets to safe places.<br>▪ Feed young children snacks.<br>▪ Open red wine.<br>▪ Put ice near drink area.<br>▪ Light candles.<br>▪ Put on music.<br>▪ Arrange food & drinks on buffet or table. |

# *Belgian Endive with Tarragon-Beet Relish*

*Belgian endive can be found in the specialty produce section of most grocery stores. It is not cheap, but a little goes a long way. This vegetable has a nice bitter crunch to it that complements the sweet roasted beets in this elegant hors d'oeuvre.*

**TARRAGON VINAIGRETTE**

⅓ cup (80 ml) vegetable oil

2 tablespoons rice vinegar

2 teaspoons chopped fresh tarragon

1 teaspoon dry mustard

½ teaspoon sugar

¼ teaspoon kosher or sea salt

¼ teaspoon ground white pepper

**BEET RELISH**

2 bunches medium beets (about 6)

2 teaspoons olive oil

1 recipe Tarragon Vinaigrette (above)

**ENDIVE BOATS**

3 heads Belgian endive

1 recipe Beet Relish (above)

*serves eight as an appetizer*

**EARLY PREPARATION:**

- Roast beets as described below. Peel, dice, and refrigerate.
- Make tarragon vinaigrette.
- Toss beets with vinaigrette.

**PROCEDURE:**

**TARRAGON VINAIGRETTE**

Whisk all ingredients together. Set aside.

**BEET RELISH**

Preheat oven to 350°F (180°C).

Trim and wash beets. Rub them with olive oil and wrap loosely in foil. Place beets on cookie sheet and roast until tender but still firm, about 40 to 50 minutes.

When cool enough to handle, peel and cut into ¼-inch (5 mm) dice, keeping them as uniform as possible.

Toss with vinaigrette and chill.

**ENDIVE BOATS**

Cut off very bottom of endive and separate leaves. When ready to serve, drain excess liquid from beets, place endive leaves on serving platter, and scoop about 1 tablespoon of beet relish onto each leaf. Serve slightly chilled.

## lascarpone Tart

*need to fuss making your own bread reat!*

*ight to ten as an appetizer*

**URE:**

**AN CRUST**

t oven to 375°F (190°C).
gether bread crumbs, Parmesan, and mly pat the mixture into the bottom 1 inch (2.5 cm) up the sides of a loose- 9 inch (23 cm) springform pan. Bake imately 10 minutes, or until the crust and crisp.

at oven to 350°F (180°C).
mascarpone cheese and blue cheese lectric mixer until smooth and creamy. one at a time, making sure egg is rporated after each addition. Mix in er sauce and white pepper. Season with sired.

filling into Parmesan crust and bake for minutes or until the top is golden brown edges are set. Remove from oven and cool. e slightly warm or at room temperature.





# Broiled Oysters with Shallot, Fennel, and Spinach Butter

**SHALLOT BUTTER**

3 shallots

1 fennel bulb

1 tablespoon olive oil

½ bunch fresh spinach, cleaned and trimmed

1 tablespoon Pernod

½ teaspoon kosher or sea salt

¼ teaspoon ground white pepper

6 tablespoons unsalted butter, room temperature

**OYSTERS**

2 dozen fresh oysters in the shell

1 recipe Shallot Butter (above)

*serves eight as an appetizer*

**EARLY PREPARATION:**

- Make Shallot, Fennel, and Spinach Butter as directed below. Wrap tightly in plastic wrap. Freeze.

**PROCEDURE:**

**SHALLOT BUTTER**

Preheat oven to 350°F (180°C).

Peel shallots and trim. Cut fennel bulb into pieces the same size as shallots. Toss shallots and fennel in olive oil and place on a cookie sheet. Bake in oven, stirring occasionally, until nicely roasted, about 30 minutes.

While vegetables are roasting, quickly dip spinach in and out of a saucepan of boiling, salted water. Squeeze dry. Chop roughly and set aside.

Purée shallots, fennel, and spinach in food processor with Pernod, salt, and pepper. Add butter and continue processing until well incorporated.

**OYSTERS**

Open oysters not more than 1 hour before serving. Store oysters belly-down on a tray of ice and cover with a moist cloth. Refrigerate.

Preheat broiler. Place oysters on a broiler pan. Dot with the Spinach, Fennel, and Shallot Butter and place under broiler for approximately 3 minutes. Serve warm.

# *Sausage-Stuffed Mushrooms*

*An interesting line-up of filling ingredients creates the terrific and unique flavo of these mushrooms.*

*serves eight as an appetizer*

**SAUSAGE STUFFING**

1 pound (450 g) white mushrooms

¼ pound (115 g) mild Italian pork sausage

1 small yellow onion, chopped

1 clove garlic, minced

2 teaspoons brandy, Marsala, or Madeira

¼ cup (30 g) bread crumbs

2 tablespoons finely chopped fresh Italian parsley

2 tablespoons finely chopped toasted almonds

¼ cup (25 g) grated mozzarella cheese

1 teaspoon kosher or sea salt

½ teaspoon freshly ground black pepper

**MUSHROOMS**

Reserved mushroom caps

1 recipe Sausage Stuffing (above)

3 tablespoons unsalted butter, room temperature

**EARLY PREPARATION:**

- Toast almonds in 350°F (180°C) oven for abo 6 to 8 minutes, until lightly brown.
- Prepare sausage stuffing as directed below.

**PROCEDURE:**

**SAUSAGE STUFFING**

Clean mushrooms and remove stems. Set mushroom caps aside to be stuffed. Finely chop stems and reserve ¼ cup.

Cook and stir sausage over medium heat.

Stir in onions and garlic and continue to cook until sausage is thoroughly cooked. Add the ¼ cup chopped mushroom stems and brandy and cook for 2 to 3 minutes. Turn off heat and stir in bread crumbs, parsley, almonds, mozzarella, salt, and pepper.

Pulse in food processor to break up the sausage, not letting it get too pasty or soft.

**MUSHROOMS**

Preheat oven to 350°F (180°C). Place approximately 1 tablespoon of stuffing in each mushroom cap and dot evenly with butter. Bake on a cookie sheet for about 10 minutes, or until heated through. Serve hot or at room temperature.





# *Creamy Blue and M*

*This simple Parmesan crust is delicious. No crumbs. Store-bought plain bread crumbs work*

*serves*

**PARMESAN CRUST**

1½ cups (180 g) bread crumbs

¾ cup (90g) grated Parmesan cheese

4 tablespoons unsalted butter, melted

**FILLING**

¾ pound (350 g) mascarpone cheese

¾ pound (350 g) blue cheese: Gorgonzola, Roquefort, Maytag blue or your personal favorite

3 eggs

½ teaspoon hot pepper sauce

¼ teaspoon ground white pepper

Salt (optional)

**PROCED**

**PARMES**

Prehe

Mix t

butter. Fi

and about

bottomed

for approx

is golden

**FILLIN**

Preh

Beat

with an

Add egg

well-inc

hot pep

salt if d

**TART**

Pou

30 to 4

and the

Ser

# *Onion Marmalade*

*Serve this fabulous preserve as an accompaniment to Creamy Blue and Mascarpone Tart (previous page).*

- 1 tablespoon olive oil
- 1 tablespoon butter
- 2 pounds (450 g) white onions, trimmed and cut into ⅛-inch thick slices
- 3 tablespoons brown sugar
- 1 tablespoon apple cider vinegar

*serves eight as an appetizer*

**PROCEDURE:**

Heat olive oil and butter in a large sauté pan. Add onions and cook over low heat stirring often until slightly caramelized, light brown in color. Stir in brown sugar and cook until onions are golden brown, about 5 more minutes. Pour in vinegar and bring to a boil. Remove from heat. Cool before serving.

# *Caramelized Pears Wrapped in Prosciutto*

*You will adore the sweet-salty flavor combination in this hors d'oeuvre.*

2 Anjou or Bartlett pears
1 tablespoon unsalted butter
1½ teaspoons sugar
24 prosciutto slices, paper thin

*serves eight as an appetizer*

**PROCEDURE:**

Slice pears in quarters and, using a small knife, remove cores. Melt butter in a large sauté pan. Add pears and sprinkle with sugar. Cook over medium heat until pears turn a deep golden color. Flip over and cook until deep golden. Transfer pears to a cookie sheet to cool. When cool enough to handle, wrap each pear section with a slice of prosciutto. Serve warm or at room temperature.

# *Fall/Winter Hors d'oeuvres* *shopping list*

*This is a complete list of ingredients you will need to make all the recipes in this menu, along with the quantity you will need for most ingredients. The menus are designed to feed a gathering of eight. If increasing or decreasing any recipes be certain to adjust quantities on the shopping list. Check your pantry before shopping, as you may already have enough of many of these items.*

**PRODUCE**

- ☐ Beets (6 medium)
- ☐ Belgian endive (3 heads)
- ☐ Fennel bulb (1)
- ☐ Garlic (1 head)
- ☐ Mushrooms, white (1 lb./450 g)
- ☐ Onions, white (1 lb./450 g)
- ☐ Onions, yellow (2)
- ☐ Pears: Anjou or Bartlett, almost ripe (3)
- ☐ Shallots (3)
- ☐ Spinach, fresh (½ bunch)

**HERBS**

- ☐ Basil, fresh (2 Tbs.)
- ☐ Parsley, fresh Italian (1 bunch)
- ☐ Tarragon, fresh (2 tsp.)

**DAIRY/EGGS**

- ☐ Butter, unsalted (¾ lb./350 g)
- ☐ Blue cheese: Gorgonzola, Roquefort, Maytag blue (¾ lb./350 g)
- ☐ Cream or half-and-half (½ cup/120 ml)
- ☐ Mascarpone cheese (¾ lb./350 g)
- ☐ Mozzarella cheese (¼ cup/25g)
- ☐ Parmesan cheese (1¼ cup/120 g)
- ☐ Eggs, large (3)

**MEAT/SEAFOOD**

- ☐ Mild Italian pork sausage (¼ lb./ 115 g)
- ☐ Prosciutto (24 slices)
- ☐ Oysters, fresh in shell (2 dozen)

**BAKING GOODS**

- ☐ Almonds (¼ cup/25 g)

**DRY GOODS**

- ☐ Bread crumbs (1¾ cups/210 g)
- ☐ Sun-dried tomatoes (2 Tbs.)
- ☐ Tortellini, ricotta- or chicken-filled (1 lb./500 g)

**CANNED GOODS**

- ☐ Chicken broth (½ cup/120 ml)

**CONDIMENTS**

- ☐ Apple cider vinegar (1 Tbs.)
- ☐ Hot pepper Sauce (½ tsp.)
- ☐ Rice vinegar (2 Tbs.)

**PANTRY STAPLES**

- ☐ Mustard, dry (1 tsp.)
- ☐ Oil, olive (3 Tbs.)
- ☐ Oil, vegetable (⅓ cup/80 ml)
- ☐ Pepper, cracked black
- ☐ Pepper, ground white
- ☐ Salt, kosher or sea
- ☐ Sugar, brown (3 Tbs.)
- ☐ Sugar, white (1½ tsp.)

**BEVERAGES**

- ☐ Brandy (2 tsp.)
- ☐ Pernod, (licorice-flavored liqueur) (1 Tbs.)
- ☐ Chardonnay
- ☐ Riesling
- ☐ Sauvignon Blanc (2 Tbs.)
- ☐ Syrah

# fall/winter formal dinner

Entertaining may seem a requirement of the season, but true entertaining is about pleasure. This classic and elegant sit-down meal will bring joy to you and your company. During this season of decreased light, let candles cast a golden warmth over your party.

While you set the standards of dress and atmosphere, the recipes included here will meet your highest standards. You'll get raves for the Horseradish Potatoes Au Gratin every time you make it, and those who see the recipe will be surprised with how easy it is to prepare. The Cured Olives and Spiced Walnuts and Pecans are unique starters and both are enjoyable to prepare. A nice touch is to make extra olives and nuts, buy decorative jars for the olives and small cellophane bags with fancy ribbons for the nuts, and present these gifts to your guests as they leave.

As your guests arrive and begin to mingle, you can offer them a glass of Chardonnay. Once your meal begins, a Cabernet is most appropriate to match the Rib Roast and Roasted Shallot-Cabernet Demi-Glace. You can also serve Meritage Red. Because this is event can be a dressy and special occasion, you should look to serve a better wine, such as one from a single vineyard or a reserve.

FALL/WINTER

# *Formal Dinner Menu*

*Spiced Walnuts and Pecans*

PAGE 64

*Lemon, Oregano, and Red Pepper Cured Olives*

PAGE 64

*Fennel-Pomegranate Salad with Lemon Dressing*

PAGE 65

*Dried Fruit and Pine Nut-Stuffed Rib Roast*

PAGE 66

*Roasted Shallot-Cabernet Demi-Glace*

PAGE 67

*Horseradish Potatoes Au Gratin*

PAGE 68

*Braised Leeks*

PAGE 69

*Chocolate-Espresso Custard*

PAGE 70

BEVERAGE SUGGESTIONS

*Chardonnay*

*Cabernet, Meritage Red*

*Photo: Dried Fruit and Pine Nut-Stuffed Rib Roast*

# Formal Dinner *planning guide*

| | **ADVANCE PREPARATIONS** | **PREP TIME** *(2 to 3 Days Ahead)* |
|---|---|---|
| **Hospitality**<br> | ▪ Create guest list. Call or send invitations.<br>▪ Provide directions if needed.<br>▪ Print shopping list & menu from www.seahillpress.com website. | ▪ Call any guests who have not responded.<br>▪ Talk to neighbors & plan parking arrangements. |
| **Shopping**<br> | ▪ Purchase pomegranate, horseradish root, olives, & items for making nuts. | ▪ Purchase beverages & groceries. |
| **Food Preparation**<br> | ▪ Clean & organize refrigerator.<br>▪ Make Spiced Walnuts & Pecans up to one week ahead. Store in airtight container at room temperature or package as individual gifts.<br>▪ Make Cured Olives. Refrigerate. | ▪ Make Lemon Dressing for salad.<br>▪ Shave Parmigiana. Refrigerate. |
| **Staging**<br> | ▪ Sketch a diagram of table set-up & placement of items.<br>▪ Plan seating arrangements.<br>▪ Plan & purchase tableware & decorations.<br>▪ Make place cards for guests.<br>▪ Borrow or purchase needed cookware & serving dishes.<br>▪ Schedule housecleaner or childcare if needed.<br>▪ Ask friends or family for specific help if needed.<br>▪ Decide what to wear. | ▪ Iron tablecloths & napkins.<br>▪ Gather, wash, & polish serving platters, utensils, dishes, & glassware.<br>▪ Set table with dinner plates, silver or flatware, glasses, salt shakers & pepper grinders. Cover with another tablecloth or sheet to keep clean.<br>▪ Confirm & communicate plans with outside help. |

*Pull out all the stops for this event, for this is a grand-scale party. These are just guidelines to help your party go as smoothly as possible. Remember that you are not bound to follow these precisely. Have fun!*

| DAY BEFORE EVENT | DAY OF EVENT | LAST TWO HOURS |
| --- | --- | --- |
| ▪ Lay place cards at dinner table. | ▪ Assist guests with last-minute questions & requests. | |
| | ▪ Purchase last-minute items: ice & flowers. | |
| ▪ Wash leeks. Refrigerate.<br>▪ Seed pomegranate. Refrigerate.<br>▪ Clean & pick over parsley sprigs for salad; chop 2 tsp. for roast.<br>▪ Chop dates, figs, & herbs for rib roast.<br>▪ Toast pine nuts for rib roast.<br>▪ Roast shallots for demi-glace. | ▪ Slice fennel for salad.<br>▪ Wash salad greens; dry well. Refrigerate.<br>▪ Assemble Horseradish Potatoes Au Gratin.<br>▪ Finish stuffing & rib roast; bake.<br>▪ Make Chocolate-Espresso Custard. | ▪ Bake Horseradish Potatoes.<br>**BEFORE SERVING:**<br>▪ Cook leeks.<br>▪ Toss salad. |
| | ▪ Chill sparkling wines, white wines, & beer.<br>▪ Set out dinner plates, tableware, & napkins.<br>▪ Prepare coffee maker. Set coffee/tea service on tray.<br>▪ Do final cleaning of kitchen & bathroom.<br>▪ Set after dinner drinks & glasses on service tray. | ▪ Try to relax - take a 20 minute siesta or do some leisurely reading.<br>▪ Shower, dress, & prepare yourself for the party!<br>▪ Move pets to safe places.<br>▪ Feed young children.<br>▪ Open red wine.<br>▪ Pour ice water in glasses.<br>▪ Light candles.<br>▪ Put on music.<br>▪ Pour creamer into pitcher.<br>▪ Arrange drinks on table. |

# *Spiced Walnuts and Pecans*

*Make more of these than you will need, because they are irresistible! You'll find them great for snacking on while you prepare for your party.*

- 1 pound (450 g) walnut halves
- 1 pound (450 g) pecan halves
- ¼ cup (60 ml) walnut oil
- 1 tablespoon ground nutmeg
- 1½ tablespoons ground ginger
- ½ teaspoon cayenne pepper
- ¼ cup (50 g) sugar
- ½ cup (120 ml) pure maple syrup
- ⅓ cup (75 ml) applejack or brandy
- 2 teaspoons sherry vinegar
- 1½ tablespoons kosher or sea salt

*makes two pounds*

**PROCEDURE:**

Preheat oven to 400°F (200°C).

Toss walnuts and pecans with walnut oil, nutmeg, ginger, cayenne, and sugar. Bake on a cookie sheet for 8 minutes.

While nuts are baking, combine maple syrup, applejack or brandy, and sherry vinegar in a small bowl.

Remove nuts from oven and toss with the syrup mixture to coat evenly. Return to oven, bake about another 5 to 8 minutes, or until you see them start to brown. Remove from oven and scrape into a large bowl. Let cool. Sprinkle with salt and toss to evenly coat.

# *Lemon, Oregano, and Red Pepper Cured Olives*

*Play with this recipe using other acidic ingredients instead of lemon, such as wine, fruit juices and flavorful vinegars. Add other herbs and spices to suit your tastes, but limit anything salty like capers or anchovies.*

- 2 pounds (1 kg) Sicilian olives (with or without pits)
- 4 teaspoons chopped fresh oregano
- 5 strips lemon zest (about 2-inches long and ¼-inch wide)
- 4 cloves garlic, minced
- 1 teaspoon whole black peppercorns
- ½ cup (120 ml) fresh lemon juice
- 2 teaspoons olive oil
- ¼ teaspoon red pepper flakes

*makes two pounds*

**PROCEDURE:**

Toss all ingredients together up to 24 hours before serving.

# *Fennel-Pomegranate Salad with Lemon Dressing*

*Pomegranate adds a festive touch to this green salad. This gorgeous fruit can keep for up to 2 months if stored in the refrigerator, so you can purchase your pomegranate early. Be sure to remove any bitter membrane that is clinging to the beautiful red pomegranate seeds. You may substitute "craisins" (dried cranberries) if pomegranate is not available.*

**LEMON DRESSING**

1 teaspoon minced garlic

2 teaspoons Dijon mustard

¼ cup (60 ml) fresh lemon juice

1 tablespoon pure maple syrup

½ cup (120 ml) vegetable oil

Pinch kosher or sea salt

Pinch ground black pepper

**FENNEL-POMEGRANATE SALAD**

2 heads Bibb (butter) lettuce

1 bunch Italian parsley

1 pomegranate

1 large fennel bulb

3 ounce (90 g) block Parmigiana cheese

1 recipe Lemon Dressing (above)

*serves eight to ten*

**EARLY PREPARATION:**

- Make Lemon Dressing in advance. Refrigerate.
- Shave Parmigiana as described below.
- Seed pomegranate. Store in refrigerator.
- Clean and pick over parsley sprigs.
- Slice fennel.
- Wash salad greens and dry between paper towels.

**PROCEDURE:**

**LEMON DRESSING**

Mix all dressing ingredients together.

**FENNEL-POMEGRANATE SALAD**

Wash and tear lettuce into bite-size pieces and place in a large salad bowl. Wash and break parsley into small pieces and add to lettuce. Remove seeds from pomegranate and mix seeds into greens. Slice fennel bulb as thinly as possible, discard tops and stalks, and add to salad mixture.

Shave cheese with a vegetable peeler to make long ribbons and scatter on salad top.

Toss with lemon dressing immediately before serving.

# *Dried Fruit and Pine Nut-Stuffed Rib Roast*

*serves eight*

**STUFFING**

¼ cup (40 g) chopped dried dates

¼ cup (40 g) chopped dried figs

¼ cup (40 g) chopped golden raisins

⅛ cup (15 g) toasted pine nuts

1 cup (125 g) small cubed dry bread crumbs

½ teaspoon chopped fresh thyme

½ teaspoon chopped fresh rosemary

1 teaspoon chopped fresh Italian parsley

Scant ½ teaspoon orange zest

⅛ teaspoon salt

¼ cup (60 ml) Riesling

¼ cup chicken stock to moisten

**ROAST AND RUB**

3 to 4 pound (1.4 kg to 2 kg) eye of rib roast or sirloin roast, have butcher fillet open

1 teaspoon chopped fresh thyme

1 teaspoon chopped fresh rosemary

1 teaspoon chopped fresh Italian parsley

1 teaspoon dry mustard

1 clove garlic, minced

Kosher or sea salt to taste

Freshly ground black pepper to taste

2 tablespoons olive oil

**EARLY PREPARATION:**

- Chop dried fruits. Wrap and store.
- Toast pine nuts in dry skillet, 2 to 3 minutes.

**PROCEDURE:**

**STUFFING**

Combine ingredients to form a thick stuffing texture.

**ROAST AND RUB**

Layer stuffing evenly into the fillet pocket of roast. Roll and tie stuffed roast.

Preheat oven to 350°F (180°C). For roast rub, stir together herbs, mustard, garlic, salt, pepper, and olive oil until blended. Thoroughly rub over roast. Bake until temperature on meat thermometer reaches 140°F (61°C), about 15 minutes per pound.

**CHEFS' TIP:**

*When you remove roast from oven, take roast out of pan and heat drippings over medium-high heat. Add Roasted Shallot Demi-Glace (next page) and let simmer in roasting pan to pick up flavor.*

# *Roasted Shallot Demi-Glace*

8 medium shallots

1 tablespoon olive oil

Kosher or sea salt to taste

Freshly ground black pepper to taste

1 clove garlic, minced

1 tablespoon butter

1½ cups (350 ml) high-quality veal stock

¼ cup (60 ml) Cabernet Sauvignon

*serves eight*

**PROCEDURE:**

To roast shallots, preheat oven to 350°F (180°C). Place shallots, olive oil, salt, and pepper into a "boat" made out of aluminum foil. Seal to completely encase, and bake for 30 minutes. This can be done well in advance. Roasted shallots can be stored in refrigerator 1 day before finishing demi-glace.

Sauté roasted shallots and garlic in butter in a sauté pan and bring to a simmer. Add veal stock and wine. Salt and pepper to taste. Turn down heat and simmer until sauce reduces, about 20 minutes. Serve over roast.

# *Horseradish Potatoes Au Gratin*

*This side dish is delicious and creamy, with a hint of heat from the horseradish. It makes a terrific accompaniment to meat, poultry, or even fish.*

- 2 cups (475 ml) heavy cream
- 1 teaspoon minced garlic
- 2 teaspoons prepared horseradish
- Pinch cayenne pepper
- 3 large baking potatoes
- Kosher or sea salt to taste
- Freshly ground black pepper to taste
- ¾ cup (170 g) grated fresh horseradish root

*serves eight*

**PROCEDURE:**

Place heavy cream, garlic, prepared horseradish, and cayenne pepper in a nonreactive saucepan and bring to a simmer. Take off heat and set aside.

Preheat oven to 400°F (200°C). Peel potatoes and slice into ⅛-inch (3 mm) rounds. Put a layer of potatoes in a 13 x 9 inch (32.5 x 23 cm) baking pan and sprinkle with salt and pepper. Sprinkle on half of the grated horseradish and then layer remaining potatoes. Season again with salt and pepper. Put remaining horseradish on top and pour on cream mixture.

Bake uncovered about 15 minutes, or until top begins to brown. Cover with foil and bake another 45 minutes until potatoes are tender. Let potatoes sit at room temperature for 10 minutes.

# *Braised Leeks*

*This name sounds so simple, but leeks make a very delicious and unique side vegetable. I discussed this dish when talking on a radio broadcast and was amazed at its popularity; numerous people called in asking for the recipe.*

8 leeks

1 tablespoon unsalted butter

16 cloves garlic

1½ cups (355 ml) chicken broth

2 teaspoons fresh lemon juice

¼ teaspoon kosher or sea salt

¼ teaspoon freshly ground black pepper

*serves eight*

**EARLY PREPARATION:**

- Wash leeks thoroughly as directed below.

**PROCEDURE:**

Cut off dark green part of leeks, about the top third. Trim the root ends and slice the leeks lengthwise. Rinse the leeks under cool running water, separating the leaves and making sure that all grit and dirt is removed. Cut leeks into 4-inch pieces, keeping layers together.

Melt butter in a large sauté pan. Add leeks to pan cut-side down. Randomly scatter garlic cloves on top of leeks. Pour chicken broth and lemon juice on top and sprinkle with salt and pepper. Cover and cook over medium heat for approximately 20 minutes, or until leeks are tender.

# *Chocolate-Espresso Custard*

*The coffee and chocolate flavors and the hint of cinnamon in these satiny custards create the perfect finish for a festive sit-down dinner.*

1¼ cups (300 ml) whole milk

1¼ cups (300 ml) heavy cream

4 tablespoons sugar

⅓ cup (75 g) cracked espresso beans

¼ teaspoon ground cinnamon

5 ounces (140 g) bittersweet chocolate

1 ounce (25 g) unsweetened chocolate

6 egg yolks

1 tablespoon Kahlúa (coffee-flavored liqueur)

2 teaspoons vanilla extract

¼ teaspoon kosher or sea salt

1 cup (240 ml) heavy cream, whipped to soft peaks

8 mint sprigs, for garnish

*serves eight*

**EARLY PREPARATION:**

- Whip 1 cup heavy cream. Store in refrigerator.

**PROCEDURE:**

Combine milk, heavy cream, sugar, espresso beans, and cinnamon in a nonreactive saucepan. Bring to just under a simmer. Remove from heat, cover, and let sit for 25 minutes.

While the mixture is steeping, melt the chocolates together over a double boiler. Make sure that the melted chocolate is uniform and free of lumps.

Whisk egg yolks in a bowl and slowly pour milk mixture into them. Slowly whisk mixture into chocolate. Add liqueur, vanilla, and salt. Place 8 (3 ounce/90 ml) soufflé or custard cups into a large pan. Strain mixture and ladle into cups. Carefully pour hot water in bottom of pan about ½ inch (1 cm) deep. Cover loosely with foil and bake approximately 30 minutes, until almost set in center but not quite. Cool in water bath.

Garnish with whipped cream and a sprig of mint. Serve chilled or at room temperature.

# *Fall/Winter Formal Dinner*
## *shopping list*

*This is a complete list of ingredients you will need to make all the recipes in this menu, along with the quantity you will need for each ingredient. The menus are designed to feed a gathering of eight. If increasing or decreasing any recipes be certain to adjust quantities on the shopping list. Check your pantry before shopping, as you may already have enough of many of these items.*

**PRODUCE**
- ☐ Fennel bulb (large)
- ☐ Garlic (3 heads)
- ☐ Horseradish root (1)
- ☐ Leeks (8)
- ☐ Lemons, for juice and zest (5)
- ☐ Lettuce: Bibb (butter) (2 heads)
- ☐ Orange, for zest (1)
- ☐ Pomegranate (1)
- ☐ Potatoes, baking (3 large)
- ☐ Shallots, medium (8)

**HERBS**
- ☐ Mint sprigs (8)
- ☐ Oregano, fresh (4 tsp.)
- ☐ Parsley, fresh Italian (1 bunch)
- ☐ Rosemary, fresh (1½ tsp.)
- ☐ Thyme, fresh (1½ tsp.)

**DAIRY/EGGS**
- ☐ Butter, unsalted (2 Tbs.)
- ☐ Whole milk (10 oz./300 ml)
- ☐ Heavy cream (34 oz./1 l)
- ☐ Parmigiana cheese, block (3 oz./90 g)
- ☐ Eggs (6)

**MEAT**
- ☐ Eye of rib or Sirloin roast, filleted (3 to 4 lbs./2 kg)

**BAKING GOODS/SPICES**
- ☐ Cayenne pepper (½ tsp.)
- ☐ Cinnamon, ground (¼ tsp.)
- ☐ Ginger, ground (1½ Tbs.)
- ☐ Nutmeg, ground (1 Tbs.)
- ☐ Red pepper flakes (¼ tsp.)
- ☐ Chocolate, bittersweet (5 oz./140 g)
- ☐ Chocolate, unsweetened (1 oz./25 g)
- ☐ Pecan halves (1 lb./450 g)
- ☐ Walnut halves (1 lb./450 g)
- ☐ Pine nuts (⅛ cup/15 g)
- ☐ Dates, dried (¼ cup/40 g)
- ☐ Figs, dried (¼ cup/40 g)
- ☐ Raisins, golden (¼ cup/40 g)
- ☐ Vanilla extract (2 tsp.)
- ☐ Walnut oil (¼ cup/60 ml)

**CANNED GOODS**
- ☐ Chicken broth (2 cups/475 ml)
- ☐ Veal stock (1½ cups/350 ml)

**DRY GOODS**
- ☐ Espresso beans (⅓ cup/75 g)
- ☐ Bread crumbs (1 cup/125 g)

**CONDIMENTS**
- ☐ Dijon mustard (2 tsp.)
- ☐ Horseradish, prepared
- ☐ Olives, Sicilian (2 lbs./2 kg)
- ☐ Pure maple syrup (½ cup/120 ml + 1 Tbs.)
- ☐ Sherry vinegar (2 tsp.)

**PANTRY STAPLES**
- ☐ Mustard, dry (1 tsp.)
- ☐ Oil, olive (4 Tbs.)
- ☐ Oil, vegetable (½ cup/120 ml)
- ☐ Peppercorns, whole black
- ☐ Salt, kosher or sea
- ☐ Sugar, white (1 cup/200 g)

**WINE**
- ☐ Riesling (¼ cup/60 ml)
- ☐ Cabernet Sauvignon (¼ cup/60 ml)
- ☐ Chardonnay
- ☐ Meritage Red

**LIQUOR**
- ☐ Applejack or brandy (⅓ cup/75 ml)
- ☐ Kahlua coffee-flavored liqueur (1 Tbs.)

# *fall/winter dessert buffet*

After a night at the theater or after a sporting event, invite a group back to your place for this delicious and elegant dessert buffet. Also, consider throwing a decadent dessert party to get your friends together to watch the Academy Awards. This menu has the advantage of being fun and a bit indulgent while having the capacity for great elegance.

We often have a hard time deciding between lemon or chocolate when ordering dessert. With this menu, you can have both, and then some. Flourless Chocolate-Pecan Cake served with a slightly contrasting Raspberry Sauce is to die for, and those who have a fondness for peanut butter will adore Caramel-Peanut Mousse Pie. Fresh seasonal fruit (we have suggested papaya with lime) balances out this impressive dessert buffet. Although available year round, papayas are prime during the fall and winter months. Be sure to purchase them early, and if they are not ripe then leave them at room temperature in a brown paper bag with a banana for a few days. You should feel a ripe papaya give the same way a ripe avocado does. Remember, a papaya with a spotty exterior but vibrant coloring will usually have more flavor.

Additionally, it is great fun to have a small selection of cheese and wine on hand for sampling. Purchase goat cheese, a blue such as Gambenzola or English Stilton, and, of course, Brie. Serve a dessert wine like a Late Harvest Riesling and Tawny Port. We also recommend serving an extra dry sparkling wine with this menu. A French-drip single bean coffee finishes this dessert buffet with great taste.

FALL / WINTER

# *Dessert Menu*

*Citrus Tart in Shortbread Pastry*

PAGE 78

*Flourless Chocolate-Pecan Cake*
*with Raspberry Sauce*

PAGE 79

*Caramel-Peanut Mousse Pie*

PAGE 80-81

*Cheese Board (Goat, Blue, and Brie)*
*Fresh Papaya and Limes*

BEVERAGE SUGGESTIONS

*Late Harvest Riesling*

*Tawny Port*

*Extra Dry Sparkling Wine*

*French-Drip Single Bean Coffee*

*Photo: Flourless Chocolate-Pecan Cake*
*with Raspberry Sauce*

# Dessert Buffet *planning guide*

| | **ADVANCE PREPARATIONS** | **PREP TIME** *(2 to 3 Days Ahead)* |
|---|---|---|
|   | ▪ Create guest list. Call or send invitations. Provide directions if needed.<br>▪ Print shopping list & menu from www.seahillpress.com website. | ▪ Call any guests who have not responded.<br>▪ Talk to neighbors & plan parking arrangements. |
|   | ▪ Review list of ingredients.<br>▪ Purchase specialty ingredients.<br>▪ Purchase ingredients for Raspberry Sauce. | ▪ Purchase beverages & groceries. |
| 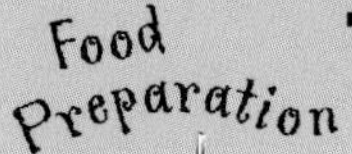   | ▪ Make Raspberry Sauce & freeze. | ▪ Store three papayas & two limes at room temperature until ripe. Refrigerate once ripened.<br>▪ Transfer Raspberry Sauce from freezer to refrigerator.<br>▪ Prepare crust for Caramel-Peanut Mousse Pie. Store loosely covered with plastic wrap at room temperature. |
|   | ▪ Sketch a diagram of seating plan, table set-up, & placement of items.<br>▪ Plan & purchase tableware and decorations.<br>▪ Borrow or purchase needed cookware & serving dishes.<br>▪ Schedule childcare if needed.<br>▪ Decide what to wear. | ▪ Gather serving platters, utensils, dishes, & glassware.<br>▪ Cover all items with plastic wrap or tablecloth to keep clean.<br>▪ Assemble centerpiece for table. |

# spring/summer brunch

After an early round of golf, Easter egg hunting, or a breathtaking morning hike, invite the party back to your place for this light brunch. Or, have a few friends over to celebrate the first day of summer by serving this delicious and very seasonal menu. This is the perfect time of year to utilize your (or your neighbors') fresh flowers and foliage. With good planning, you can prepare much of this menu in advance and leave yourself free to enjoy the day.

Have a small tray of cut-up vegetables waiting for your guests when they arrive. If your brunch is following a morning activity, they may be hungry and need a little something to hold them over till brunch is served. You only need a little time to grill the skewers and broil the tomatoes, and everything else is done ahead.

Serve a chilled and refreshing brut sparkling wine as your guests arrive. For the main meal, serve a Merlot to match the flavors of the Greek-Style Lamb Skewers. Sauvignon Blanc would go nicely with the Herb and Hazelnut-Stuffed Tomatoes. For dessert, serve Late Harvest Riesling with the Kirsch-Splashed Berries.

SPRING/SUMMER

# *Brunch Menu*

*Greek-Style Lamb Skewers*

PAGE 88

*Herb and Hazelnut-Stuffed Tomatoes*

PAGE 89

*Sweet Onion-Thyme Tart*

PAGE 90-91

*Kirsch-Splashed Berries*
*with Brown Sugar Shortbread*

PAGE 92-93

BEVERAGE SUGGESTIONS

*Brut Sparkling Wine*

*Merlot*

*Sauvignon Blanc*

*Late Harvest Riesling*

*Photo: Greek-Style Lamb Skewers*

# Brunch *planning guide*

| ADVANCE PREPARATIONS | PREP TIME *(2 to 3 Days Ahead)* |
|---|---|
|   ▪ Create guest list. Call or send invitations.<br>▪ Provide directions if needed.<br>▪ Print shopping list from www.seahillpress.com website. | ▪ Call any guests who have not responded.<br>▪ Talk to neighbors & plan parking arrangements. |
|   ▪ Review list of ingredients.<br>▪ Purchase ingredients for Brown Sugar Shortbread. | ▪ Purchase beverages & non-perishable groceries (not berries). |
|    ▪ Clean & organize refrigerator.<br>▪ Make Brown Sugar Shortbread up to one week in advance. Store in airtight container at room temperature. | ▪ Slice onions for Onion Tart. Cut onion for lamb into wedges.<br>▪ Pull frozen puff pastry for Onion Tart from freezer to refrigerator.<br>▪ Make marinade for lamb. Cut lamb into chunks. |
|   ▪ Sketch a diagram of table set-up & placement of items. Plan seating arrangements.<br>▪ Plan & purchase tableware & decorations.<br>▪ Borrow or purchase needed cookware & serving dishes.<br>▪ Schedule childcare if needed.<br>▪ Ask friends or family for specific help if needed.<br>▪ Decide what to wear. | ▪ Gather, wash, & polish serving platters, utensils, dishes, & glassware.<br>▪ Cover items with plastic wrap or tablecloth to keep clean. |

*This menu of fresh foods and natural colors really suits warm weather; you won't be cooking over a hot stove on the day of the party. These are just guidelines to help your party go as smoothly as possible. Remember that you are not bound to follow these precisely. Have fun!*

| DAY BEFORE EVENT | DAY OF EVENT | LAST TWO HOURS |
|---|---|---|
| | ▪ Assist guests with last-minute questions & requests. | |
| ▪ Purchase berries. | ▪ Go to store for last-minute items: ice & flowers. | |
| ▪ Toast hazelnuts for Stuffed Tomatoes.<br>▪ Crumble cheese for tomatoes.<br>▪ Chop basil & parsley for tomatoes, & thyme for tart.<br>▪ Caramelize onions for tart.<br>▪ Marinate lamb. | ▪ Stuff tomatoes. (Don't broil until the last minute.)<br>▪ Bake tart.<br>▪ Clean berries for Kirsch-Splashed Berries. | **BEFORE SERVING:**<br>▪ Broil tomatoes.<br>▪ Barbecue lamb skewers.<br>▪ Toss berries with kirschwasser. |
| ▪ Clean house. Iron tablecloths & napkins.<br>▪ Confirm arrangements with outside help.<br>▪ Set-up buffet area & seating.<br>▪ Arrange centerpieces & décor. | ▪ Chill white wines.<br>▪ Set out dinner plates, tableware, & napkins.<br>▪ Prepare coffee maker. Set coffee/tea service on tray.<br>▪ Do final cleaning of kitchen & bathroom. | ▪ Try to relax - take a 20 minute siesta or do some leisurely reading.<br>▪ Move pets to safe places.<br>▪ Feed young children snacks.<br>▪ Shower, dress, & prepare yourself for the party!<br>▪ Open red wine.<br>▪ Pour juice into pitcher.<br>▪ Light candles.<br>▪ Put on music.<br>▪ Pour creamer in pitcher.<br>▪ Arrange food & drinks on buffet or table. |

# *Greek-Style Lamb Skewers*

*These traditional kabobs are made in the Greek shish kabob style with lamb. You could, if you prefer, use beef or even chicken. As for me, lamb and spring just seem to go together!*

**GREEK MARINADE**

3 cloves garlic, minced

1 tablespoon oregano

Kosher or sea salt to taste

Freshly ground black pepper to taste

2 tablespoons olive oil

2 tablespoons fresh lemon juice (1 lemon)

¼ cup (60 ml) Zinfandel

**SKEWERED LAMB**

1 recipe Greek Marinade (above)

3 pounds (900 g) boneless leg of lamb, cut into 1-inch (2.5 cm) cubes

2 onions, chopped into large cubes or wedges

8 metal skewers

*serves eight*

**EARLY PREPARATION:**

- Make Greek Marinade as described below.
- Trim any excess fat off outside of leg of lamb and then cut into 1-inch (2.5 cm) chunks. Store meat in refrigerator in dish you will be using for marinating.
- Peel onion and cut into 8 wedges, leaving the root end intact so that onion wedges stay together. Store in refrigerator in a plastic bag or covered container.

**PROCEDURE:**

**GREEK MARINADE**

Mix all marinade ingredients together.

Store in refrigerator in a tightly sealed container until ready to use.

**SKEWERED LAMB**

Mix marinade, meat, and onions together well. Marinate lamb and onion cubes in a covered container overnight.

Preheat barbecue grill. Thread lamb and onion chunks alternately onto skewers, putting about 3 pieces of lamb on each skewer. Reserve marinade for basting.

Barbecue skewers over medium-hot coals for about 4 minutes total, turning and basting frequently with reserved marinade. Discard any unused marinade.

# *Herb and Hazelnut-Stuffed Tomatoes*

*This offers a magnificent combination of flavors and textures: crunchy hazelnuts, sweet basil, and juicy tomatoes with creamy, tangy blue cheese.*

⅔ cup (60 g) hazelnuts, toasted and skins removed

4 large vine-ripened tomatoes

2 tablespoons finely chopped fresh basil

3 tablespoons finely chopped fresh Italian parsley

2 cloves garlic, minced

½ cup (2 ounces/50 g) crumbled blue cheese

⅛ teaspoon kosher or sea salt

⅛ teaspoon ground white pepper

*serves eight*

**EARLY PREPARATION:**

- Toast hazelnuts as directed below and store tightly covered.
- Chop basil and parsley and store in refrigerator, tightly covered.

**PROCEDURE:**

To toast hazelnuts, preheat oven to 375°F (180°C). Spread hazelnuts on a cookie sheet and bake for 10 to 12 minutes, shaking sheet periodically. Remove from oven and while hazelnuts are still warm, place them in a dry, clean kitchen towel and vigorously rub them together, removing the tough outer skin. Chop roughly by hand or in a food processor.

Preheat broiler, with rack in second highest position. Remove core from tomatoes, taking care not to cut too deeply. Cut tomatoes in half horizontally. Cut off a very small portion on the bottom of each half, just enough so it stands upright without rolling. Scoop out seeds with a spoon, taking care not to remove the tomato flesh.

Combine hazelnuts, basil, parsley, garlic, blue cheese, salt, and pepper in a small bowl. Spoon mixture into tomato halves, packing it into tomato crevices. Place tomatoes mixture-side up onto a cookie sheet.

Broil about 4 inches from broiler for 3 to 4 minutes. When cheese begins to gently bubble tomatoes are done. Remove and serve immediately.

**CHEFS' NOTES:**

*There's still hope in this recipe for those who don't eat nuts. Simply substitute toasted bread crumbs for the hazelnuts. It's a different, but wholly satisfying, alternative! Scout out the best tomatoes for this recipe (you're truly blessed if you can pick them from your own garden!).*

# *Sweet Onion-Thyme Tart*

*Caramelizing onions to a deep golden brown intensifies the flavor and makes for a robust, delicious filling.*

**CARAMELIZED ONIONS**

2 tablespoons unsalted butter

2½ pounds (1 kg) sweet onions (such as Walla Walla or Vidalia), thinly sliced

⅛ teaspoon kosher or sea salt

⅛ teaspoon freshly ground black pepper

**CHEFS' NOTES:**

*Try to be patient when caramelizing the onions. You really need to take it slow and develop that beautiful golden brown without any black specks or they will become bitter. The onions only need a stir every once in a while so there is no need to baby-sit them, just plan on being home for a while and check on them every now and then.*

*serves eight*

**EARLY PREPARATION:**

- Slice onions and store in a tightly-sealed container in the refrigerator.
- Thaw pastry, 2 hours at room temperature or overnight in refrigerator.

**PROCEDURE:**

**CARAMELIZED ONIONS**

Melt butter in a large heavy skillet over medium heat. Add onions and stir to coat with butter. Turn heat to low and cover, stirring occasionally to be sure onions are not sticking. Continue to cook until onions have become a deep golden color; this may take an hour or more. Add salt and pepper.

Refrigerate for later use or keep at room temperature if making the tart right away.

*Continued on next page.*

# Sweet Onion-Thyme Tart

*Continued from previous page.*

**PUFF PASTRY**

1 (1 pound/450 g) package frozen puff pastry, thawed

**ONION-THYME FILLING**

1 cooked Puff Pastry shell (previous page)

2 eggs

1 cup sour cream

1 recipe Caramelized Onions (previous page)

½ teaspoon kosher or sea salt

¼ teaspoon freshly ground black pepper

1 teaspoon chopped fresh thyme

**PUFF PASTRY**

Roll out puff pastry on a lightly-floured work surface to form an 11½-inch (29 cm) diameter round to fit in a 10½-inch (26.5 cm) greased tart pan with a removable bottom. You may have to trim the edges with a knife to accomplish this. Refrigerate for 1 hour.

Preheat oven to 425°F (220°C). Prick pastry shell with a fork in a dozen places and cover with aluminum foil. Fill the shell with pie weights or dry beans and bake in the center of oven for about 12 minutes. Remove the foil and weights and continue to bake until the pastry is cooked through and just slightly golden, about another 5 minutes. Remove shell from oven. Leave oven on if immediately baking tart.

**ONION-THYME FILLING**

Place tart pan on a cookie sheet. Whisk together eggs, sour cream, caramelized onion mixture, salt, pepper, and thyme in a medium bowl. Pour into prepared tart shell and bake in center of oven until tart is golden and slightly puffed, about 20 to 25 minutes. When done, the mixture will no longer appear loose in the middle. Remove from oven. When cool enough, remove outer ring of tart pan. Serve slightly warm.

# *Kirsch-Splashed Berries with Brown Sugar Shortbread*

*The kirsch adds a nice zing to the berries. Using brown sugar in the shortbread gives it a wonderful texture with a bit of a crunch.*

**BROWN SUGAR SHORTBREAD**

½ cup (100 g) light brown sugar

2 sticks (1 cup/225 g) unsalted butter, room temperature

½ teaspoon salt

2 cups all-purpose flour

**CHEFS' TIP:**

*If not serving right away, store shortbread in an airtight container between layers of waxed paper for up to 1 week.*

*serves eight*

**PROCEDURE:**

**BROWN SUGAR SHORTBREAD**

Preheat oven to 250°F (120°C). Spread brown sugar on a cookie sheet and place in oven until dry and hard, about 8 to 10 minutes. Cool and put into food processor or blender and process until fine and powdery. Set aside.

Beat butter with an electric mixer until it is light and fluffy. Slowly add brown sugar and continue to beat until fully incorporated. Blend salt and flour together, and add about ½ cup at a time to butter mixture. Stop mixer and scrape down sides after each addition. Continue to mix for a couple more minutes until dough is smooth and soft.

Shape dough into a ball. Set ball in the center of a parchment-lined cookie sheet. Roll dough with a rolling pin into an 8 inch (20 cm) circle about ½ inch (1 cm) thick, using an 8 inch (20 cm) cake pan or pie tin as a guide. Cut off any excess dough. Press around the edge with a fork to create a decorative border. Score the shortbread into 8 wedges. Cover tightly with plastic wrap and refrigerate for at least 2 hours and up to 4 days.

Preheat oven to 325°F (165°C). Put shortbread in oven and reduce heat to 300°F (150°C). Bake for 15 minutes then rotate pan around halfway to assure even baking. Bake another 15 minutes. Remove shortbread from oven and cool pan on a rack for 5 minutes. Remove shortbread from cookie sheet and continue to cool on rack.

*Continued on next page.*

# *Kirsch-Splashed Berries*

*Continued from previous page.*

**BERRIES**

4 pints (1.8 kg) fresh seasonal berries (blueberries, raspberries, strawberries, blackberries)

3 tablespoons kirschwasser liqueur

**PROCEDURE:**

**BERRIES**

Wash and trim berries. Place berries in large bowl and sprinkle with kirsch. Toss gently. Serve with shortbread on the side.

**CHEFS' TIP:**

*Kirschwasser is a colorless liqueur distilled from wild cherries used to flavor confectionery and pastry. It is sometimes just called kirsch. Quite strong, but a wonderful addition to baked goods. Indulge and buy it—it lasts forever.*

# *Spring/Summer Brunch* *shopping list*

*This is a complete list of ingredients you will need to make all the recipes in this menu, along with the quantity you will need for each ingredient. The menus are designed to feed a gathering of eight. If increasing or decreasing any recipes be certain to adjust quantities on the shopping list. Check your pantry before shopping, as you may already have enough of many of these items.*

### PRODUCE

- ☐ Berries: Your choice of blueberries, raspberries, strawberries, blackberries (4 pints/1.8 kg)
- ☐ Garlic (1 head)
- ☐ Lemons, for juice (2)
- ☐ Tomatoes, large vine-ripened (4)
- ☐ Onions, large yellow (2)
- ☐ Onions, sweet: Walla Walla, Vidalia (2½ lbs./1 kg)

### HERBS

- ☐ Basil, fresh (2 Tbs.)
- ☐ Oregano, fresh (1 Tbs.)
- ☐ Parsley, fresh Italian (3 Tbs.)
- ☐ Thyme, fresh (1 tsp.)

### MEAT

- ☐ Lamb, boneless leg (3 lbs./1.5 kg)

### DAIRY/EGGS

- ☐ Blue cheese (2 oz./50 g)
- ☐ Butter, unsalted (¾ lb./350 g)
- ☐ Sour cream (1 cup/240 ml)
- ☐ Eggs (2)

### BAKING GOODS

- ☐ Hazelnuts (⅔ cup/60 g)

### FROZEN FOODS

- ☐ Puff pastry (1 lb./450 g)

### PANTRY STAPLES

- ☐ Oil, olive (2 Tbs.)
- ☐ Flour, all-purpose (2 cups)
- ☐ Salt, kosher or sea
- ☐ Peppercorns, black for grinding
- ☐ Pepper, ground white
- ☐ Sugar, light brown (4 oz./100 g)

### LIQUOR

- ☐ Kirschwasser liqueur (3 Tbs.)

### WINE

- ☐ Sparkling wine, brut
- ☐ Late Harvest Riesling
- ☐ Merlot
- ☐ Sauvignon Blanc

### SUPPLIES

- ☐ Removable-bottom tart pan
- ☐ Metal skewers (8)

# spring/summer buffet

When you think of a spring or summer buffet, you think of being outside on a sunny deck, mingling with friends, and eating what you like, when you like. This menu is versatile, as all of the dishes taste fantastic served either warm or at room temperature. This flexibility leaves you plenty of time to enjoy your own party, and to savor your culinary efforts.

Your guests will adore the spicy-sweet combination of Chile-Rubbed Turkey with Green Apple Sauce. And even the vegetable-phobic will relent once they try the addictive Chilled Asparagus with White Bean-Tomato Vinaigrette. If a guest wants to contribute something to the party, you can ask for a dessert. Or serve Kirsch-Splashed Berries with Brown Sugar Shortbread from the spring/summer brunch menu on pages 92 to 93, though those with a sweet tooth won't be disappointed by the dessert-like flavor of Creamy Corn Custard.

You won't need much decorative color because this menu is quite colorfully balanced, from the green of the asparagus and avocado to the red of the turkey and salmon. Think about placing a few corn husks around the serving table or dishes to add atmosphere.

Because you are likely to serve this menu on a hot day, you'll want to serve chilled wines. Wines that work very well chilled are Riesling, Sauvignon Blanc, Chardonnay, and Zinfandel. For a red, serve Merlot. Also, cool drinks like lemonade, flavored iced teas, and sparkling apple cider are wonderful non-alcoholic choices to pair with Chile-Rubbed Turkey.

SPRING/SUMMER

# *Buffet Menu*

*Thai Cilantro Shrimp*
*with Avocado and Tomato Salsa*

PAGE 100-101

*Seattle-Style Barbecued Salmon*

PAGE 102

*Asparagus with White Bean-Tomato Vinaigrette*

PAGE 103

*Chile-Rubbed Turkey Breast*
*with Green Apple Sauce*

PAGE 104-105

*Creamy Corn Custard*

PAGE 106

BEVERAGE SUGGESTIONS

*Riesling*

*Sauvignon Blanc*

*Chardonnay, Zinfandel*

*Merlot*

*Lemonade, Iced Tea*

*Sparkling Apple Cider*

*Photo: Thai Cilantro Shrimp*
*with Avocado and Tomato Salsa*

# Buffet planning guide

| | ADVANCE PREPARATIONS | PREP TIME *(2 to 3 Days Ahead)* |
|---|---|---|
|  | ▪ Create guest list. Call or send invitations.<br>▪ Provide directions if needed.<br>▪ Print shopping list & menu from www.seahillpress.com website. | ▪ Call any guests who have not responded.<br>▪ Talk to neighbors & plan parking arrangements. |
|  | ▪ Review list of ingredients.<br>▪ Purchase specialty ingredients (chipolte chiles) & those for barbecue sauce. | ▪ Purchase beverages & all groceries. |
|  | ▪ Clean & organize refrigerator.<br>▪ Make barbecue sauce for salmon up to two weeks ahead. | ▪ Make chipotle rub for turkey. Refrigerate.<br>▪ Prepare Green Apple Sauce. Refrigerate.<br>▪ Make Sweet Chili Dressing for salsa.<br>▪ Make White Bean-Tomato Vinaigrette for asparagus. Refrigerate |
|  | ▪ Sketch a diagram of table set-up & placement of items. Plan seating arrangements.<br>▪ Plan & purchase tableware & decorations.<br>▪ Borrow or purchase needed cookware & serving dishes.<br>▪ Schedule childcare if needed.<br>▪ Ask friends or family for specific help if needed.<br>▪ Decide what to wear. | ▪ Gather, wash, & polish serving platters, utensils, dishes, & glassware.<br>▪ Cover items with plastic wrap or tablecloth to keep clean. |

*So much of this menu can be prepared ahead of time that the day of the party is a breeze. These are just guidelines to help your party go as smoothly as possible. Remember that you are not bound to follow these precisely. Have fun!*

| DAY BEFORE EVENT | DAY OF EVENT | LAST TWO HOURS |
|---|---|---|
| | ▪ Assist guests with last-minute questions & requests. | |
| | ▪ Go to store for last-minute items such as ice. | |
| ▪ Marinate shrimp.<br>▪ Put rub on turkey breast.<br>▪ Shuck corn & cut from cob. Refrigerate.<br>▪ Trim and blanch asparagus in salted water; drain well. Refrigerate. | ▪ Finish Avocado & Tomato Salsa. Refrigerate. | **BEFORE SERVING:**<br>▪ Make Creamy Corn Custard and bake.<br>▪ Grill or bake turkey.<br>▪ Grill shrimp.<br>▪ Warm Green Apple Sauce.<br>▪ Broil salmon.<br>▪ Drizzle vinaigrette over asparagus. |
| ▪ Clean house or party site. Iron tablecloths & napkins.<br>▪ Confirm arrangements with outside help.<br>▪ Set-up buffet & seating areas. | ▪ Chill white wines & beer.<br>▪ Set out dinner plates, tableware, & plenty of napkins.<br>▪ Do final cleaning of kitchen & bathroom. | ▪ Try to relax - take a 20 minute siesta or do some leisurely reading.<br>▪ Move pets to safe places.<br>▪ Feed snacks to young children.<br>▪ Shower, dress, & prepare yourself for the party!<br>▪ Open red wine.<br>▪ Pour juice into pitcher.<br>▪ Light candles.<br>▪ Put on music.<br>▪ Put ice near drink area.<br>▪ Arrange food & drinks on buffet or table. |

# *Thai Cilantro Shrimp*

*This recipe uses two really fun ingredients: Thai sweet chili sauce and pickled ginger. I like to use Thai sweet chili sauce in marinades, salad dressings, and sauces. It has a wonderfully sweet flavor with just a hint of heat. Pickled ginger is beautiful and has a flavor subtle enough to use as a garnish. Minced, it acts as a unique fresh seasoning.*

⅓ cup (75 ml) vegetable oil

⅓ cup (75 ml) Thai sweet chili sauce

¼ cup minced cilantro

2 tablespoons minced pickled ginger

5 cloves garlic, minced

1½ pounds (675 g) large (21-25 count) raw shrimp, peeled and deveined

*serves eight*

**PROCEDURE:**

Combine oil, sweet chili sauce, cilantro, pickled ginger, and garlic in a large, low-sided glass or ceramic baking dish. Add shrimp and toss well. Cover tightly and put in refrigerator the day before serving. Stir once or twice.

Preheat barbecue grill or broiler. Cook shrimp over high heat on the barbecue grill or in broiler for about 3 minutes total, turning once. Transfer to a platter and serve either warm or cold, accompanied by Avocado and Tomato Salsa on next page.

# *Avocado and Tomato Salsa*

**SWEET CHILI DRESSING**

3 tablespoons rice vinegar

2 tablespoons Thai sweet chili sauce

1½ teaspoons Dijon mustard

⅓ cup (75 ml) vegetable oil

**AVOCADO AND TOMATO SALSA**

1 large vine-ripened tomato

1 large avocado

3 green onions, white and green parts, finely chopped

¼ teaspoon kosher or sea salt

¼ freshly ground black pepper

2 teaspoons fresh lime juice

1 recipe Sweet Chili Dressing (above)

**EARLY PREPARATION:**

- Make dressing in advance as directed below and store in a tightly covered container in refrigerator.

**PROCEDURE:**

**SWEET CHILI DRESSING**

In a mini processor or blender, combine vinegar, chili sauce, and mustard. Slowly drizzle remaining oil in a thin stream to create a creamy, emulsified dressing.

**AVOCADO AND TOMATO SALSA**

Core and halve tomato and remove most of the seeds. Cut into tiny ⅛- to ¼-inch (3 to 5 mm) diced pieces. Peel avocado and remove pit. Dice avocado flesh small. Mix tomato and avocado in a medium-size bowl with green onions, salt, pepper, lime juice and Sweet Chili Dressing. Serve salsa on a platter surrounded by Thai Cilantro Shrimp (previous page).

# *Seattle-Style Barbecued Salmon*

*The addition of coffee is what makes this intensely flavored barbecue sauce "Seattle Style." Adding just a small amount of coffee gives the sauce a delicious and distinct flavor. Save a little from your morning brew.*

**BARBECUE SAUCE**

1 tablespoon unsalted butter

⅔ cup (75 g) diced yellow onion (about 1 medium onion)

1 teaspoon minced garlic

3 Roma tomatoes, peeled, seeded, and diced

2 tablespoons ketchup

1 tablespoon Dijon mustard

1 tablespoon brown sugar

2 teaspoons pure maple syrup

¼ teaspoon cayenne

2 teaspoons ancho chile powder*

½ teaspoon pasilla chile powder*

2 teaspoons paprika

½ teaspoon ground cumin

2 teaspoons Worcestershire sauce

2 tablespoons brewed coffee

**can use all ancho for a milder sauce or common chili powder if ancho and pasilla are unavailable.*

**SALMON**

1 (2 pound/2 kg) boned, skinned salmon fillet

1 recipe Barbecue Sauce (above)

*makes about 2½ cups*

**EARLY PREPARATION:**

- Prepare Barbecue Sauce up to 2 weeks ahead and refrigerate.
- Remove skins from tomatoes by putting them into boiling water for 1 minute.
- Brew coffee, or save some from your morning coffee and put into a sealed container in the refrigerator.

**PROCEDURE:**

**BARBECUE SAUCE**

Melt butter in a medium saucepan over low heat. Add onions and garlic and cook until translucent, 3 to 5 minutes. Add tomatoes and simmer for 10 minutes. Stir in remaining ingredients and simmer for 20 more minutes, stirring occasionally.

Purée mixture in a food processor and refrigerate.

**SALMON**

Preheat broiler, first adjusting one oven rack to uppermost position, about 3 to 4 inches (8 to 10 cm) from heat source, and positioning the second rack in the middle of oven.

Line a cookie sheet with aluminum foil. Place salmon fillet skin-side down on the cookie sheet.

Broil salmon fillet on upper rack for about 6 minutes. Take salmon out of oven and evenly spread barbecue sauce on top. You may choose not to use the entire amount of sauce: it is quite intense! Put salmon back in oven on middle rack and continue to broil for another 4 to 5 minutes. Serve warm.

# *Asparagus with White Bean-Tomato Vinaigrette*

*Don't limit this to a side dish. For a complete and satisfying meal, add a little shrimp or poached chicken and some Bibb lettuce. It's great any time of year.*

**WHITE BEAN-TOMATO VINAIGRETTE**

⅓ cup (75 ml) sherry vinegar

1 teaspoon Dijon mustard

2 teaspoons pure maple syrup

1½ teaspoons minced shallots

⅓ cup (75 g) canned white beans

1 tablespoon tomato paste

¼ teaspoon kosher salt

¼ teaspoon black pepper

¾ cup (175 ml) peanut oil

**ASPARAGUS**

2 teaspoons kosher or sea salt

2½ pounds (1.25 kg) fresh asparagus, trimmed of woody stems

1 recipe White Bean-Tomato Vinaigrette (above)

*makes 1¼ cups*

**EARLY PREPARATION:**

- Make vinaigrette in advance as described below. Chill in refrigerator in a covered container for up to 1 week.
- The day before serving you may trim or snap off woody end of asparagus; blanch as described below. Refrigerate.

**PROCEDURE:**

**WHITE BEAN-TOMATO VINAIGRETTE**

Mix all ingredients except oil together in a blender or food processor. Slowly drizzle in oil while machine is running to create a smooth, emulsified dressing. Chill.

**ASPARAGUS**

Bring 1½ quarts (1.4 l) water and salt to a boil in a large heavy-bottomed pan with lid. Add asparagus to the boiling water. Cover and simmer for 1 to 2 minutes, depending on the size of asparagus; thicker spears may take longer to cook. Remove from boiling water and immediately immerse in ice water. When cool, drain well.

Place asparagus on a serving platter and drizzle with White Bean-Tomato Vinaigrette just before serving.

# *Chile-Rubbed Turkey Breast*

*This rub will give a deliciously crisp finish to the turkey breast. If time permits, refrigerate the turkey for 24 hours before cooking and serving. If necessary, you can shorten this time down, but do try to give it at least 2 hours to achieve the full intensity of flavor. Serve this with Green Apple Sauce to balance out the spiciness!*

**CHILE RUB**

⅓ cup (75 ml) puréed canned chipotle chiles

1 teaspoon chili powder

¼ cup olive oil

½ teaspoon kosher or sea salt

½ teaspoon freshly ground black pepper

⅛ teaspoon granulated sugar

**TURKEY**

2½ to 3 pounds (1.25 kg) raw turkey breast

**CHEFS' TIP:**

*Chipotle ("chih-POHT-lay") chiles come canned and I usually find them with the Mexican ingredients at the supermarket. A chipotle is a smoked jalapeño so it is quite hot and intensely flavored. If you and your guests have milder taste preferences, cut down on the amount of chipotle in the marinade. The smoky flavor it adds is quite nice and complimentary to the tart Green Apple Sauce.*

*serves eight*

**EARLY PREPARATION:**

- Make chile rub in advance and refrigerate.
- Coat turkey breast with chile rub. Refrigerate for 24 hours.

**PROCEDURE:**

**CHILE RUB**

Purée the chipotle chiles in a food processor. If you buy them in adobo sauce, take the chiles out of the sauce, but don't be too concerned about wiping them free of sauce.

Blend chiles, chili powder, olive oil, salt, pepper, and sugar together.

NOTE: Remember to wear gloves or otherwise guard your hands when cutting the chiles—on tiny cuts, the chile oils feel as spicy as they taste! If you can't locate these chiles, you can try substituting a puréed chile sauce, such as Sambal Oelek, and cut the amount in half.

**TURKEY**

Coat turkey breast with chile rub. Refrigerate for 24 hours.

Preheat barbecue grill or preheat oven to 350°F (180°C).

Barbecue over low heat or roast in oven for approximately 40 to 50 minutes, until internal temperature in the center reaches 165°F (75°C) and the juices run clear.

# *Green Apple Sauce*

*The tangy flavor of this dish gives a refreshing balance to the Chile-Rubbed Turkey Breast on your spring or summer buffet table. This Green Apple Sauce is nothing like the applesauce you grew up with, but rather a flavorful, gourmet spin on an old tradition.*

1 tablespoon olive oil

1 tablespoon minced shallot

1 Granny Smith apple, peeled, cored and cut into ½ inch (1 cm) pieces

1 (12 ounce/350 ml) can frozen apple juice concentrate

⅓ cup (80 ml) lime juice

2 cups (475 ml) chicken broth

3 tablespoons light brown sugar

2 tablespoons unsalted butter

*makes about 1½ cups*

**EARLY PREPARATION:**

- This can be made in advance and refrigerated for up to 4 days. Gently warm immediately before serving.

**PROCEDURE:**

Heat olive oil in a medium saucepan. Add minced shallot and apples. Cook over medium-high heat stirring occasionally for about 5 minutes. Add apple juice concentrate, lime juice, chicken broth, and brown sugar. Reduce slowly at a simmer to about 1½ cups, this may take 30 to 40 minutes. Purée and strain well, pushing most of the solids through strainer. Return sauce to pan. Whisk in butter while still slightly warm.

**CHEFS' TIP:**

*If you can find a can of green apple juice concentrate in the store, buy it! If using green apple juice, reduce lime juice to 1 tablespoon.*

# Creamy Corn Custard

*If corn is a comfort food for you, then this is the homemade summer-in-the-country corn dish you've been looking for! It's really worth the extra effort to scrape the cob and remove all the milky liquid.*

6 ears fresh corn, husked with silk removed

1 tablespoon unsalted butter, for greasing

2 tablespoons olive oil

¼ cup (60 g) minced onion

1½ teaspoons kosher salt

1 teaspoon light brown sugar

¼ teaspoon ground cayenne

1 cup (240 ml) heavy cream

1 cup (240 ml) whole milk

4 eggs, lightly beaten

2 teaspoons cornstarch

*serves eight*

**EARLY PREPARATION:**

- Shuck corn and cut from cob as described below. Refrigerate.

**PROCEDURE:**

Cut corn off cob directly into a bowl to save juices. With back of knife, scrape cobs into bowl to extract even more juice.

Adjust oven rack to lower-middle of oven and preheat to 350°F (180°C). Bring 1 quart (1 l) of water to boil in a saucepan or teakettle. Butter a 2 quart (2 l) casserole.

Heat a large heavy-bottomed skillet over medium-high heat and add olive oil. Add corn kernels and onion and cook, stirring occasionally, for about 5 minutes. Add salt, brown sugar, and cayenne. Stir in heavy cream and cook, stirring occasionally, until thickened, about 5 minutes. Transfer to a large bowl and stir in milk, then whisk in eggs and cornstarch.

Pour mixture into buttered casserole dish and place in a large roasting pan. Pour boiling water into roasting pan, surrounding casserole. Carefully place pan in oven and bake about 35 to 40 minutes. The top should be brown and bubbly, and the center only slightly soft. Remove casserole dish from roasting pan and cool 5 to 10 minutes before serving.

# *Spring/Summer Buffet* shopping list

*This is a complete list of ingredients you will need to make all the recipes in this menu, along with the quantity you will need for each ingredient. The menus are designed to feed a gathering of eight. If increasing or decreasing any recipes be certain to adjust quantities on the shopping list. Check your pantry before shopping, as you may already have enough of many of these items.*

**PRODUCE**

☐ Apple, Granny Smith (1)
☐ Asparagus (2½ lbs./1.25 kg)
☐ Avocado (1 large)
☐ Cilantro, fresh (1 bunch/25 g)
☐ Corn, sweet (6 ears)
☐ Garlic (1 head)
☐ Limes, for juice (6)
☐ Onions, green (3)
☐ Onion, yellow (2 medium)
☐ Shallots (2 large)
☐ Tomato, vine-ripened (1 large)
☐ Tomatoes, Roma (3)

**POULTRY/FISH**

☐ Turkey breast, raw (2½-3 lbs./1.25 kg)
☐ Salmon fillet (2 lbs./2 kg)
☐ Shrimp, large (21-25 count) (1½ lbs./675 g)

**DAIRY/EGGS**

☐ Butter, unsalted (4 Tbs.)
☐ Heavy cream (1 cup/240 ml)
☐ Whole milk (1 cup/240 ml)
☐ Eggs (4)

**SPICES**

☐ Ancho chile powder (2 tsp.)
☐ Cayenne (½ tsp.)
☐ Chili powder (1 tsp.)
☐ Cumin, ground (½ tsp.)
☐ Paprika (2 tsp.)
☐ Pasilla chile powder (½ tsp.)

**CANNED GOODS**

☐ Chicken broth (2 cups/475 ml)
☐ Chipotle chiles (⅓ cup/75 ml puréed)
☐ Tomato paste (1 Tbs.)
☐ White beans (1 14-oz./400 g can)

**CONDIMENTS**

☐ Dijon mustard (2 Tbs.)
☐ Ketchup (2 Tbs.)
☐ Peanut oil (¾ cup/175 ml)
☐ Pickled ginger (2 Tbs. minced)
☐ Rice vinegar (3 Tbs.)
☐ Sherry vinegar (⅓ cup/75 ml)
☐ Thai sweet chili sauce (½ cup/120 ml)
☐ Worcestershire sauce (2 tsp.)

**FROZEN FOODS**

☐ Apple juice concentrate, regular or green (1 12-oz./350 ml can)

**DRY GOODS**

☐ Coffee (for brewing 2 Tbs.)

**PANTRY STAPLES**

☐ Cornstarch (2 tsp.)
☐ Oil, olive (½ cup/120 ml)
☐ Oil, vegetable (⅔ cup/150 ml)
☐ Pure maple sugar (4 tsp.)
☐ Sugar, brown (4 Tbs.)

**WINE**

☐ Chardonnay
☐ Merlot
☐ Riesling
☐ Sauvignon Blanc
☐ Zinfandel

# *spring/summer picnic*

*t*his is a simple menu with fewer elements, making it easy to take to the beach or the pool. As long as the weather permits, we would chose to eat outdoors over inside anytime. Have a basket ready to make it easy to head out to the park for dinner. A basket would contain a citronella candle to keep pests away, matches, a wine and bottle opener, a wine bag, either to keep white wine cold or to keep the red from getting too hot, moist toilettes, a blanket, and a wide-mouthed thermal container for soups. Also keep the necessary eating utensils and plates close by. You can buy neat plastic wine goblets or small juice glasses quite cheaply, and they are durable and don't topple easily on a rocking boat, hilly lawn, or rocky beach.

This menu has a perfect balance between the fresh and light Lentil Gazpacho with Shrimp and the Grilled Zucchini and Tomato Salad, and the somewhat decadent Italian Cheese and Ham Torta and buttery Incredible Oatmeal Cookies. Consider serving soup in something fun, like small mason jars, teacups, or glass, china, or pottery bowls.

Decorate along with the theme and location of your party. If you're at a baseball game, bring along team pennants or hats, or find some wildflowers in your team's colors and throw them in a baseball glove for the table. To keep bugs at bay, light a citronella in a simple metal pail and set near food. Don't forget to bring a trash bag. Bring along blankets or beach towels for sitting (or impromptu water fights) and sunscreen to battle the elements. If you've got a large beach umbrella, bring it along and set it to maximize your guests' sitting area. Cover food with mesh domes made just for this, or use thin fabric such as netting, lace, or voile.

For this fresh and easy picnic party, throw a chilled Riesling, Chenin Blanc, and a bottle of Zinfandel into the basket. Also, a pale ale or a wheat beer will taste fantastic when served with this menu.

SPRING / SUMMER

# *Picnic Menu*

*Lentil Gazpacho with Shrimp*

PAGE 114

*Grilled Zucchini Salad with Tomatoes and Fresh Basil*

PAGE 115

*Italian Cheese and Ham Torta*

PAGE 116

*Incredible Oatmeal Cookies*

PAGE 117

BEVERAGE SUGGESTIONS

*Riesling*

*Chenin Blanc*

*Sauvignon Blanc*

*Zinfandel*

*Pale Ale or Wheat Beer*

*Photo: Grilled Zucchini Salad with Tomatoes and Fresh Basil*

# Picnic *planning guide*

| | ADVANCE PREPARATIONS | PREP TIME *(2 to 3 Days Ahead)* |
|---|---|---|
| Hospitality | ▪ Reserve picnic location.<br>▪ Create guest list. Call or send invitations.<br>▪ Provide directions if needed.<br>▪ Print shopping list & menu from www.seahillpress.com website. | ▪ Call any guests who have not responded.<br>▪ Confirm your meeting spot & parking plans. |
| Shopping  | ▪ Review list of ingredients.<br>▪ Purchase specialty ingredients. | ▪ Purchase beverages & all non-perishable groceries. |
| Food Preparation  | ▪ Clean & organize refrigerator. | ▪ Make Incredible Oatmeal Cookies. Store at room temperature. |
| Staging  | ▪ Sketch a diagram of table set-up & placement of items. Plan seating arrangements.<br>▪ Borrow or purchase needed cookware, serving dishes, portable seating & tables, & portable stereo.<br>▪ Schedule childcare if needed.<br>▪ Ask friends or family for specific help if needed.<br>▪ Decide what to wear. | ▪ Gather, wash, & polish serving platters, utensils, dishes, & glassware.<br>▪ Cover items with plastic wrap or tablecloth to keep clean.<br>▪ Gather & wash containers for transporting food. |

*There's so little to do as far as food preparation on the day of your picnic; simply double-check that you have everything packed and leave the house on time to enjoy the glorious day. These are just guidelines to help your party go as smoothly as possible. Remember that you are not bound to follow these precisely. Have fun!*

| DAY BEFORE EVENT | DAY OF EVENT | LAST TWO HOURS |
|---|---|---|
| | ▪ Assist guests with last-minute questions & requests. | |
| | ▪ Go to store for last-minute items: bread for soup & ice. | |
| ▪ Prepare dough for torta.<br>▪ Make gazpacho; do not add shrimp. Refrigerate.<br>▪ Grate cheeses and dice ham for torta. Refrigerate.<br>▪ Chop parsley for torta & zucchini salad, about 1¼ cups. Refrigerate.<br>▪ Make dressing for salad. Refrigerate. | ▪ Finish torta. Leave at room temperature for up to 3 hours. | ▪ Finish zucchini salad.<br>▪ Garnish gazpacho with shrimp. |
| ▪ Chill white wines & beer.<br>▪ Confirm arrangements with outside help.<br>▪ Pack serving dishes & utensils, tableware, napkins, cups, portable seating & tables, portable stereo & music. | ▪ Pack chilled white wines & beer.<br>▪ Shower, dress, & prepare yourself for the party! | ▪ At Picnic Site: Open red wine. |

# *Lentil Gazpacho with Shrimp*

1 cup (100 g) lentils, cooked (about 1½ cups cooked)

1½ cups (350 g) chopped fresh Roma tomatoes

½ cup (115 g) finely diced onion

1 green bell pepper, finely chopped

½ cup (115 g) finely chopped, peeled, and seeded cucumber

1 jalapeño, finely minced

2 cloves garlic, minced

48 ounces (1.4 l) tomato juice

¼ cup (60 ml) fresh lime juice

¼ teaspoon paprika

2 teaspoons chopped fresh dill

2 teaspoons chopped fresh basil

¼ teaspoon kosher or sea salt

¼ teaspoon freshly ground black pepper

½ pound (225 g) cooked bay shrimp

*serves eight to ten*

**EARLY PREPARATION:**

- Prepare gazpacho in advance and refrigerate.
- Garnish with shrimp just before serving.

**PROCEDURE:**

Mix all ingredients together, except for shrimp, and chill. Serve with shrimp on top as garnish.

# *Grilled Zucchini Salad with Tomatoes and Fresh Basil*

**BASIL DRESSING**

¼ cup (60 ml) balsamic vinegar

3 cloves garlic, minced

⅓ cup (75 g) chopped fresh basil

⅓ cup (75 g) chopped fresh Italian parsley

1 teaspoon kosher or sea salt

¼ teaspoon freshly ground black pepper

¼ cup (60 ml) olive oil

**ZUCCHINI SALAD**

8 zucchini, cut into ¼-inch (5 mm) angled rounds

¼ cup (60 ml) olive oil

½ teaspoon kosher or sea salt

¼ teaspoon freshly ground black pepper

6 vine-ripened tomatoes, cored and cut into 6 wedges

1 recipe Basil Dressing (above)

*serves eight*

**EARLY PREPARATION:**

- Chop parsley.
- Make dressing in advance.

**PROCEDURE:**

**BASIL DRESSING**

Mix all dressing ingredients together.

**ZUCCHINI SALAD**

Heat barbecue grill to medium-high. Lay out zucchini rounds on a platter. Mix together olive oil, salt, and pepper and brush onto zucchini rounds. Grill about 1 minute on each side and lay on a cookie sheet to cool.

Toss together zucchini, tomatoes, and dressing 30 minutes before serving. Serve at room temperature or slightly chilled.

# Italian Cheese and Ham Torta

**EGG CRUST**

3 cups (480 g) all-purpose flour

¼ cup (50 g) sugar

1 teaspoon kosher or sea salt

½ teaspoon ground white pepper

1 teaspoon baking powder

1½ sticks (¾ cup/175 g) unsalted butter, chilled

3 eggs

**TORTA FILLING**

2 pounds (900 g) ricotta cheese

6 eggs

1 teaspoon freshly ground black pepper

½ cup (50 g) grated fresh Parmesan cheese

¾ pound (340 g) mozzarella, coarsely grated

1 pound (450 g) ham, diced small

½ cup (50 g) chopped fresh Italian parsley

1 recipe Egg Crust (above)

**CHEFS' TIP:**

*This torta can be kept at room temperature for up to 3 hours, or refrigerate for up to 1 day and let come to room temperature before serving.*

*serves ten to twelve*

**EARLY PREPARATION:**

- Grate Parmesan cheese.
- Grate mozzarella.
- Dice ham.
- Mince parsley.

**PROCEDURE:**

**EGG CRUST**

Butter an 11 x 17 inch (28 x 43.5 cm) jelly-roll pan and set aside.

Combine flour, sugar, salt, white pepper, and baking powder in the bowl of a food processor and pulse several times. Distribute butter evenly over the dry ingredients and pulse again until fine. Add eggs and continue to pulse until the dough forms a ball. Remove the dough and press into a rough rectangle shape about 2-inches (5 cm) thick. Refrigerate or freeze.

Lightly flour a work surface and roll dough to fit buttered jelly-roll pan; fold dough in quarters to transfer easily to pan. Bring dough all the way up edges of pan.

**TORTA FILLING**

Position oven rack to lower third of oven and preheat to 350°F (180°C).

Put ricotta in a large bowl and whisk until smooth. Stir in eggs 1 at a time. Add remaining filling ingredients.

Pour filling into pastry-lined jelly-roll pan and smooth top. Bake for 35 to 40 minutes or until filling is golden brown and top of filling is just set. Rotate pan halfway through baking time.

# *Incredible Oatmeal Cookies*

- 1½ sticks (¾ cup/175 g) unsalted butter, room temperature
- ¼ cup (50 g) shortening
- ½ cup (100 g) granulated sugar
- ½ cup (100 g) brown sugar
- 1 cup (160 g) all-purpose flour
- 2 cups (450 g) quick-cooking oats
- 1 teaspoon baking soda
- ¾ teaspoon kosher or sea salt
- ⅛ teaspoon nutmeg
- 1½ teaspoons vanilla extract

*makes about two dozen cookies*

**PROCEDURE:**

Preheat oven to 350°F (180°C). Grease a cookie sheet with butter or nonstick cooking spray. Beat butter, shortening, sugar, and brown sugar with an electric mixer until creamy. Add flour, oats, baking soda, salt, nutmeg, and vanilla. Blend well.

Lightly flour hands. Scoop up about 2 tablespoons of dough using a small spoon, and gently roll it between the palms of your hands to form a small ball. Place dough about 2 inches (5 cm) apart on cookie sheet. Using the palm of your hand, press lightly on each ball to flatten it out into a ¼-inch (3 mm) thick round.

Bake in oven on middle rack for about 10 minutes. Cookies should be just a little golden brown around the edges. Cool cookies on baking sheet.

**STORAGE:**

Transfer cooled cookies to airtight container for storing. Freeze for up to 2 weeks, or at room temperature for 3 days.

# *Spring/Summer Picnic* *shopping list*

*This is a complete list of ingredients you will need to make all the recipes in this menu, along with the quantity you will need for each ingredient. The menus are designed to feed a gathering of eight. If increasing or decreasing any recipes be certain to adjust quantities on the shopping list. Check your pantry before shopping, as you may already have enough of many of these items.*

### PRODUCE

- ☐ Cucumber (1)
- ☐ Garlic (1 head)
- ☐ Limes, for juice (3 to 4)
- ☐ Tomatoes, Roma (about 6)
- ☐ Tomatoes, vine-ripened (6)
- ☐ Onion, yellow (1 medium)
- ☐ Pepper, green bell (1)
- ☐ Pepper, jalapeño (1)
- ☐ Zucchini, small (8)

### HERBS

- ☐ Basil, fresh (½ cup)
- ☐ Dill, fresh (2 tsp.)
- ☐ Parsley, fresh Italian (1 bunch/1 cup)

### DAIRY/EGGS

- ☐ Butter, unsalted (1 lb./500 g)
- ☐ Mozzarella cheese (¾ lb./150 g)
- ☐ Parmesan cheese, fresh (2 oz./50 g)
- ☐ Ricotta cheese (2 lbs./900 g)
- ☐ Eggs (9)

### MEAT/SEAFOOD

- ☐ Shrimp, bay (½ lb./225 g)
- ☐ Ham (1 lb./450 g)

### SPICES/EXTRACTS

- ☐ Paprika (¼ tsp.)
- ☐ Nutmeg (⅛ tsp.)
- ☐ Vanilla extract (1½ tsp.)

### DRY GOODS

- ☐ Lentils, dried (1 cup/180 g)
- ☐ Oats, quick-cooking (2 cups/450 g)

### CONDIMENTS

- ☐ Balsamic vinegar (¼ cup/60 ml)

### BEVERAGES

- ☐ Tomato juice (48 oz./1.5 l)

### PANTRY STAPLES

- ☐ Baking powder (1 tsp.)
- ☐ Baking soda (1 tsp.)
- ☐ Flour, all-purpose (4 cups/640 g)
- ☐ Oil, olive (½ cup/120 ml)
- ☐ Pepper, whole black
- ☐ Pepper, ground white
- ☐ Salt, kosher or sea
- ☐ Shortening (¼ cup/50 g)
- ☐ Sugar, brown (½ cup/100 g)
- ☐ Sugar, white granulated (¾ cup/150 g)

### WINE/BEER

- ☐ Chenin Blanc
- ☐ Riesling
- ☐ Sauvignon Blanc
- ☐ Zinfandel
- ☐ Pale ale or wheat beer

### SUPPLIES

- ☐ Wide-mouth soup container

# spring/summer hors d'oeuvres

This Asian inspired hors d'oeuvres party is much more than appetizers, and is really quite filling. You can chose just a few of the items if the party is scheduled for midday. It also makes for a fun after-theater meal on a hot summer evening.

We think the twist on some traditional Asian dishes are really fun. Asian-Style Avocado and Shrimp on Artichoke Leaves are as delicious as they are beautiful and unusual. Tobiko, used in this recipe, is the roe of flying fish and has an orange-red color, mild flavor, and slight crunch. Available in most Asian grocery stores and grocery store sushi bars, it is worth seeking out for this dish because its sparkly fresh color makes a beautiful presentation. My favorite sushi-chef is always happy to sell me a couple of tablespoons.

Using the tenderloin of pork instead of an inferior cut of meat produces a more elegant Barbecued Pork than the common dish found in many Chinese-American restaurants. Create a condiment bar to go along with the pork. Dress up a table with Asian-inspired décor and arrange the Sesame Salt, Peanut Sauce, toasted sesame seeds, mustard, and cocktail sauce. If available, bring out white porcelain ware, celedon dishes, lacquered trays and chopsticks, and bamboo mats. This menu would look beautiful if written in caligraphy. Display the menu in a beautiful black or bamboo frame on your serving area. Decorate by placing a variety of colored and clear bowls with floating votive candles around your deck and house. For splendor and grace, buy a single, beautiful orchid to reign in a vase on your most central table.

The fresh flavors of Asian fusion food work well with Sauvignon Blanc. For a red wine, the spicy characters of Syrah and Zinfandel blend perfectly with spicy foods.

SPRING/SUMMER

# *Hors d'oeuvres Menu*

*Green Onion Pancakes*

*Sesame Salt*

PAGE 124-125

*Marinated Cucumber Spears*

PAGE 125

*Shrimp and Vegetable Rice Paper Rolls*

*Peanut Sauce*

PAGE 126-127

*Kalbi-Style Short Ribs*

PAGE 127

*Asian-Style Avocado and Shrimp*

*On Artichoke Leaves*

PAGE 128

*Barbecued Pork Tenderloin*

PAGE 129

BEVERAGE SUGGESTIONS

*Sauvignon Blanc,*

*Zinfandel, Syrah*

*Photo: Shrimp and Vegetable Rice Paper Rolls with Peanut Sauce*

# Hors d'oeuvres *planning guide*

| | ADVANCE PREPARATIONS | PREP TIME *(2 to 3 Days Ahead)* |
|---|---|---|
| Hospitality  | ▪ Create guest list. Call or send invitations.<br>▪ Provide directions if needed.<br>▪ Print shopping list & menu from www.seahillpress.com website. | ▪ Call any guests who have not responded.<br>▪ Talk to neighbors & plan parking arrangements. |
| Shopping  | ▪ Purchase specialty ingredients: Mirin.<br>▪ Purchase ingredients for Sesame Salt. | ▪ Purchase beverages & all groceries. |
| Food Preparation  | ▪ Clean & organize refrigerator.<br>▪ Make Sesame Salt up to 1 week ahead.<br>▪ Purchase Tobiko up to 1 week ahead. Refrigerate. | ▪ Steam artichokes. Refrigerate.<br>▪ Make Asian sauce for Asian-Style Avocado.<br>▪ Make marinade for Cucumber Spears.<br>▪ Prepare Peanut Sauce.<br>▪ Make marinade & marinate pork tenderloin.<br>▪ Prepare Kalbi rib marinade. |
| Staging  | ▪ Sketch a diagram of table set-up & placement of items. Plan seating arrangements.<br>▪ Plan & purchase tableware & decorations.<br>▪ Borrow or purchase needed cookware & serving dishes.<br>▪ Schedule housecleaner or childcare if needed.<br>▪ Decide what to wear. | ▪ Gather, wash, & polish serving platters, utensils, dishes, & glassware.<br>▪ Cover items with plastic wrap or tablecloth to keep clean. |

*A beautiful Asian spread of this caliber is enhanced with condiments and garnishes. Lucky for you, advanced planning gives you time to spend on presentation. These are just guidelines to help your party go as smoothly as possible. Remember that you are not bound to follow these precisely. Have fun!*

| DAY BEFORE EVENT | DAY OF EVENT | LAST TWO HOURS |
|---|---|---|
| | ▪ Assist guests with last-minute questions & requests. | |
| | ▪ Go to store for last-minute items: ice, flowers. | |
| ▪ Toast sesame seeds for pancakes & pork.<br>▪ Make mustard & ketchup sauces for Barbecued Pork.<br>▪ Bake Barbecued Pork.<br>▪ Marinate Kalbi ribs.<br>▪ Mince green onions & cilantro for pancakes.<br>▪ Prepare all ingredients for Rice Paper Rolls. | ▪ Assemble Rice Paper Rolls.<br>▪ Cut & marinate Cucumber Spears for 4 hours. | ▪ Slice Barbecued Pork & arrange on serving platter with condiments.<br>▪ Prepare Green Onion Pancake dough.<br>**BEFORE SERVING:**<br>▪ Cook Green Onion Pancakes.<br>▪ Finish Asian-Style Avocado & Shrimp.<br>▪ Cook ribs. |
| ▪ Clean house or party site. Iron tablecloths & napkins.<br>▪ Confirm arrangements with outside help.<br>▪ Set-up buffet & seating areas. | ▪ Arrange flowers & décor.<br>▪ Chill white wines & beer.<br>▪ Set out tableware & plenty of cocktail napkins.<br>▪ Do final cleaning of kitchen & bathroom. | ▪ Try to relax — take a 20 minute siesta or do some leisurely reading.<br>▪ Move pets to safe places.<br>▪ Feed snacks to young children.<br>▪ Shower, dress, & prepare yourself for the party!<br>▪ Open red wine.<br>▪ Pour juice into pitcher.<br>▪ Put ice near drink area.<br>▪ Light candles.<br>▪ Put on music.<br>▪ Arrange food & drinks on buffet or table. |

# *Green Onion Pancakes*

*With a chewy texture and exotic seasonings these will not last long on your hors d'oeuvres buffet!*

4 cups (640 g) all-purpose flour

1½ cups (350 ml) boiling water

⅓ cup (80 ml) sesame oil

⅓ cup (40 g) minced green onions (green and white parts)

⅓ cup (40 g) minced cilantro

⅓ cup (40 g) sesame seeds, lightly toasted

1¼ cups (300 ml) peanut oil, for frying

1 recipe Sesame Salt (next page)

*serves eight*

**EARLY PREPARATION:**

- Mince green onions; refrigerate in plastic bag.
- Mince cilantro; refrigerate in plastic bag.
- Lightly toast sesame seeds by placing them on a cookie sheet and baking in a preheated 350°F (180°C) oven for about 7 to 8 minutes.

**PROCEDURE:**

Place flour in a large bowl and add boiling water, stir until a shaggy dough forms. Gather dough into a ball and knead on a floured board until soft, about 5 minutes.

Cover dough with a damp towel and let rest for 15 minutes. Knead another 5 minutes.

Roll dough into a long cylinder about 2 inches (5 cm) wide. Cut into 8 equal pieces. Using a rolling pin, roll 1 piece into a 6-inch (15 cm) round. Brush top with sesame oil and sprinkle with ¼ teaspoon sesame salt, ½ tablespoon green onions, ½ tablespoon cilantro, and 2 teaspoons sesame seeds.

Roll up pancake tightly, stretching to lengthen it slightly. Tie ends of cylinder around as if forming a knot. Flatten knotted ball on a lightly floured surface with palm of your hand and then roll it out again into a 6-inch (15 cm) round. Repeat with remaining dough.

In a large heavy skillet, pour enough peanut oil to come to a depth of ¼ inch (5 mm). Heat oil to 380°F (195°C), a cube of bread will turn golden after 15 seconds. Fry only a couple of pieces at a time until both sides are golden, 2 to 3 minutes per side. Drain on paper towels and sprinkle with sesame salt. Cut each into 4 triangles. Serve hot.

# *Sesame Salt*

*Use this seasoning on any Asian-inspired dish that calls for regular salt.*

1 tablespoon sesame seeds, lightly toasted

2 teaspoons kosher or sea salt

½ teaspoon ground white pepper

*serves eight*

**EARLY PREPARATION:**

- Toast sesame seeds as directed on previous page.

**PROCEDURE:**

Put ingredients into a spice grinder or mini-food processor and pulse until coarsely ground.

# *Marinated Cucumber Spears*

*Crispy and refreshing!*

**MARINADE**

⅔ cup (150 ml) rice vinegar

¼ cup (50 g) sugar

1½ teaspoon soy sauce

1 pinch red pepper flakes

**CUCUMBER**

1 English cucumber

*serves eight*

**PROCEDURE:**

**MARINADE**

For marinade, mix together rice vinegar, sugar, soy sauce, and pepper flakes.

**CUCUMBER**

Trim ends of cucumber and cut cucumber into 3 sections, about 6-inch (15 cm) lengths each. Cut each section in half lengthwise and then each of the halves into 3 spears.

Place cucumbers in a shallow baking dish and pour marinade over top. Marinate cucumber spears in the refrigerator 4 hours before serving. Serve upright in a fancy glass or vase.

# *Shrimp and Vegetable Rice Paper Rolls*

12 (21-25 count) raw shrimp, peeled and deveined

1 cup rice or bean thread vermicelli noodles, softened in hot water and drained

1 tablespoon rice vinegar

Pinch salt

2 green onions, cut in very thin 1-inch (2.5 cm) strips (green and white parts)

2 carrots, grated

12 fresh mint leaves, washed and cut in half lengthwise

½ cup cilantro leaves, washed

½ head red leaf lettuce, cleaned and the tender outer leaves cut in 2- by 3-inch (5- by 7.5-cm) rectangular pieces

12 8-inch (20 cm) round rice paper sheets

*makes twelve rolls*

**EARLY PREPARATION:**

- Peel and devein shrimp. Cook as described below. Refrigerate.
- Cool, drain, and cut shrimp. Refrigerate in a sealed container.
- Immerse noodles in hot water; drain and refrigerate.
- Cut green onions. Refrigerate.
- Grate carrots. Refrigerate.
- Wash and cut mint leaves. Refrigerate.
- Wash cilantro leaves and pick off small sprigs. Refrigerate.
- Wash lettuce and cut tender outer leaves into 2 by 3 inch (5 by 7.5 cm) pieces.

**PROCEDURE:**

Gently cook shrimp in salted water until just cooked through. Plunge into cold water to stop the cooking and then drain well. Cut shrimp in half lengthwise through the middle and refrigerate until ready to use.

Soften noodles by immersing them in VERY hot water until soft and tender to the bite. Drain well and toss with rice vinegar and salt.

Immerse rice paper rounds in VERY hot water until pliable, about 35 to 45 seconds. Shake off excess liquid and place all 12 on work surface.

Inside the middle of the rice paper rounds, lay two halves of shrimp, pink-side down. To fill and roll think "burrito-style." Distribute noodles, green onions, carrots, mint, cilantro, and lettuce evenly. Roll paper as tightly as you can, taking care not to rip the rice paper, folding in the ends halfway through rolling. Place on serving dish shrimp-side up. They will show through paper for a beautiful presentation. If rolls are tightly wrapped they can be cut in half and placed filling-side up on plate for an even more stunning presentation. Serve with Peanut Sauce (next page).

# *Peanut Sauce*

- ½ teaspoon chili powder
- ½ teaspoon cayenne pepper
- 2 teaspoons minced fresh garlic
- 2 tablespoons minced fresh ginger
- ½ cup (115 ml) creamy peanut butter
- ⅓ cup (80 ml) soy sauce
- 2 tablespoons sugar
- 2 tablespoons rice vinegar
- 2 tablespoons water
- 1 tablespoon sesame oil
- ½ cup (120 ml) vegetable oil

*makes about 1½ cups*

**PROCEDURE:**

Put chili powder, cayenne, garlic, ginger, peanut butter, soy sauce, sugar, vinegar, and water (all ingredients except oils) into blender. Put blender lid on tightly. Turn blender on low and carefully take off lid while machine is still running. Very slowly pour in sesame and vegetable oil to create a creamy consistency.

# *Kalbi-Style Short Ribs*

*I love the lightness of this teriyaki-style marinade. It gives the ribs terrific flavor without a sticky glaze.*

**MARINADE**

- 2 cloves garlic, minced
- 2 teaspoons grated fresh ginger
- 1 cup (240 ml) light soy sauce
- ¾ cup (175 ml) Mirin
- 2 tablespoons dark brown sugar
- 2 tablespoons honey
- ⅛ teaspoon red pepper flakes

**SHORT RIBS**

2½ pounds (2 kg)
Kalbi-style short ribs (ask your butcher to cut them for you if not available in the case.)

*serves eight*

**PROCEDURE:**

**MARINADE**

Mix all marinade ingredients together.

**SHORT RIBS**

Place short ribs in a large, shallow glass or ceramic baking dish and marinate for 24 hours.

Preheat barbecue grill or broiler. Barbecue over medium-high heat, about 2 minutes per side, or broil 2 to 3 minutes per side.

**CHEFS' TIP:**

*Mirin is a Japanese sweet cooking rice wine, you'll find it available in the Asian section of most grocery stores.*

# *Asian-Style Avocado and Shrimp On Artichoke Leaves*

**ARTICHOKES**

2 medium artichokes

**ASIAN SAUCE**

2 egg yolks

¼ cup (30 ml) chicken broth

1 tablespoon rice vinegar

1 tablespoon Mirin (Japanese sweet cooking rice wine)

1 tablespoon sugar

1½ teaspoon soy sauce

1 teaspoon fresh lemon juice

Pinch cayenne pepper

**AVOCADO AND SHRIMP**

2 avocados, ripe but firm

3 green onions, finely chopped

¼ cup (15 g) finely chopped cilantro

½ pound (225 g) bay shrimp

1 recipe Asian Sauce (above)

1 ounce (30 g) Tobiko (optional)

*serves eight*

**EARLY PREPARATION:**

- Steam artichokes, as described below. Pull off leaves and refrigerate.
- Make sauce in advance and set aside for up to 1 hour before serving or refrigerate for up to 2 days for later use.

**PROCEDURE:**

**ARTICHOKES**

Steam artichokes until tender. Pull off leaves while still slightly warm. (Use the middle leaves as opposed to the outer leaves which are tough and small or the inner leaves which are tender and prickly). Lay artichoke leaves on a serving platter.

**ASIAN SAUCE**

Combine sauce ingredients in a double boiler and whisk over medium heat until sauce is the consistency of thin mayonnaise. Strain immediately through a fine sieve into a bowl and stir so that the mixture cools quickly.

**AVOCADO AND SHRIMP**

Dice avocado small and mix gently with onions, cilantro, and shrimp (all other ingredients except Tobiko.) Fold in sauce. Place a small mound of filling on the bottom part of the artichoke leaf. Garnish with Tobiko if using.

# *Barbecued Pork Tenderloin*

*Feel free to skip the food coloring in this recipe; its purpose is strictly visual. It's here to create the red coloring we are accustomed to when ordering this appetizer in Chinese-American restaurants. By omitting the food coloring you still end up with a nice crisp exterior and juicy, moist center.*

**CONDIMENTS**

½ cup (50 g) sesame seeds, toasted

2 tablespoons dry mustard, mixed with enough cool water to form a paste

¼ cup (60 ml) ketchup, mixed with 2 teaspoons prepared horseradish and 1 teaspoon Worcestershire sauce

**BARBECUED PORK**

2 tablespoons Hoisin sauce

4 tablespoons light soy sauce

1 tablespoon dry sherry

½ teaspoon kosher or sea salt

¼ cup (60 ml) sugar

½ teaspoon red food coloring (optional)

2 pork tenderloins, trimmed of any visible fat

*serves eight*

**EARLY PREPARATION:**

**CONDIMENTS**

- Toast sesame seeds by heating in a small dry pan and stirring until light brown, about 2 minutes.
- Prepare mustard and store tightly covered.
- Mix ketchup, horseradish, and Worcestershire sauce and store in the refrigerator, tightly covered, until ready to serve.

**PROCEDURE:**

**BARBEQUED PORK**

Mix together Hoisin, soy sauce, sherry, salt, sugar, and food coloring, if using. Add trimmed whole pork tenderloins and marinate for 24 hours, turning at least once.

Preheat oven to 350°F (180°C).

Place pork on a roasting pan and bake for about 30 minutes, turning over after 15 minutes, or until thermometer reaches 150°F (66°C).

Cool and slice on the bias into ¼-inch thick slices. Shingle slices on a serving platter. Serve pork with small bowls of sesame seeds, mustard, and cocktail sauce (above).

# *Spring/Summer Hors d'oeuvres shopping list*

*This is a complete list of ingredients you will need to make all the recipes in this menu, along with the quantity you will need for each ingredient. The menus are designed to feed a gathering of eight. If increasing or decreasing any recipes be certain to adjust quantities on the shopping list. Check your pantry before shopping, as you may already have enough of many of these items.*

### PRODUCE
- ☐ Artichokes (2 medium)
- ☐ Avocados, ripe but firm (2)
- ☐ Carrots (2)
- ☐ Cucumber, English (1)
- ☐ Garlic (1 head)
- ☐ Ginger (¼ lb./225 g piece)
- ☐ Green onions (2 bunches)
- ☐ Lemon, for juice (1)
- ☐ Lettuce, red leaf (½ head)

### HERBS
- ☐ Mint leaves (12)
- ☐ Cilantro (1 large bunch)

### EGGS
- ☐ Eggs (2)

### MEAT/POULTRY/SEAFOOD
- ☐ Kalbi-style short ribs (2½ lbs./2 kg; ask your butcher to cut them for you if not available in the case.)
- ☐ Pork tenderloins (2)
- ☐ Shrimp, bay (½ lb./225 g)
- ☐ Shrimp, raw (12 x 21-25 count)
- ☐ Tobiko (1 oz./30 g) (optional)

### BAKING GOODS
- ☐ Cayenne pepper (¾ tsp.)
- ☐ Chili powder (½ tsp.)
- ☐ Dry mustard (2 Tbs.)
- ☐ Red pepper flakes (¼ tsp.)
- ☐ Red food coloring (optional) (½ tsp.)
- ☐ Sesame seeds (1 cup/100 g)

### CANNED GOODS
- ☐ Chicken broth (¼ cup/30 ml)

### CONDIMENTS
- ☐ Honey (2 Tbs.)
- ☐ Horseradish, prepared (2 tsp.)
- ☐ Ketchup (¼ cup/60 ml)
- ☐ Peanut butter, creamy (½ cup/115 g)
- ☐ Rice vinegar (1 cup/240 ml)
- ☐ Worcestershire sauce (1 tsp.)

### ASIAN SPECIALTY SECTION
- ☐ Hoisin sauce (2 Tbs.)
- ☐ Mirin - Japanese sweet cooking rice wine (1 cup/240 ml)
- ☐ Noodles, rice or bean thread vermicelli (1 cup/200 g)
- ☐ Rice paper rounds (12 x 8 inch/ 20 cm)
- ☐ Soy sauce (½ cup/120 ml)
- ☐ Soy sauce, light (1¼ cups/300 ml)

### PANTRY ITEMS
- ☐ Flour, all-purpose (4 cups/640 g)
- ☐ Oil, peanut oil (1¼ cups/300 ml)
- ☐ Oil, sesame oil (½ cup/120 ml)
- ☐ Oil, vegetable oil (½ cup/120 ml)
- ☐ Sugar, dark brown (2 Tbs.)
- ☐ Sugar, white granulated (¾ cup/150 ml)
- ☐ Salt, kosher or sea
- ☐ Ground white pepper

### WINE
- ☐ Dry sherry (1 Tbs.)
- ☐ Sauvignon Blanc
- ☐ Syrah
- ☐ Zinfandel

# spring/summer formal dinner

This is the meal of the season, the one that you will all remember for its grace and taste. Serving a formal sit-down dinner can often be quite intimidating. This menu makes it very easy to plate each course and serve everyone at the same time, including yourself! Create a large central centerpiece, or consider placing small, simple flower arrangements at each place setting. A champagne flute can work nicely as a vase for this.

Because the soup is cold, and should be made ahead, your first course is prepared long before your guests arrive. Save some room in the fridge for soup bowls or cups so that your chilled soup can be served in a proper vessel. The Vodka-Spiked Tomato Sauce, cake filling, and dessert sauce should also be done at least the day before the party. If your guests' preferences don't lean toward seafood, this menu is as delicious using chicken breasts instead of halibut, and omitting the shrimp in the asparagus still produces a wonderful vegetable side.

As this event is a bit more formal than your average gathering, you'll want to go for the big guns: choose a single vineyard Chardonnay to wash down this seafood extravaganza. A late harvest wine or an ice wine also will also go well. Ice wine is a delicious treat that tastes almost like fresh juice, and will be a welcome refresher on a warm summer evening. If you would like to have a red wine on hand, try a fruity Pinot Noir, Syrah, or Merlot.

SPRING/SUMMER

# *Formal Dinner Menu*

*Gougères*

PAGE 136

*Chilled Cucumber-Curry Soup*

PAGE 137

*Grilled Halibut Fillet*
*with Vodka-Spiked Tomato Sauce*

PAGE 138

*Herbed Basmati Rice Pilaf*

PAGE 139

*Steamed Asparagus*
*with Lemon Bay Shrimp and Brown Butter*

PAGE 140

*Basque Strawberry-Rhubarb Cake*
*with Almond Crème Anglaise*

PAGE 141-143

BEVERAGE SUGGESTIONS

*Sparkling Blanc de Blancs,*
*Chardonnay, Sauvignon Blanc, Ice Wine,*
*Pinot Noir, Syrah, or Merlot*

*Photo: Chilled Cucumber-Curry Soup*

# Formal Dinner *planning guide*

| | ADVANCE PREPARATIONS | PREP TIME *(2 to 3 Days Ahead)* |
|---|---|---|
| Hospitality  | ▪ Create guest list. Call or send invitations.<br>▪ Provide directions if needed.<br>▪ Print shopping list & menu from www.seahillpress.com website.<br>▪ Make place cards for guests. | ▪ Call any guests who have not responded.<br>▪ Talk to neighbors & plan parking arrangements. |
| Shopping  | ▪ Review list of ingredients. | ▪ Purchase beverages & groceries (except fish). |
|  Food Preparation | 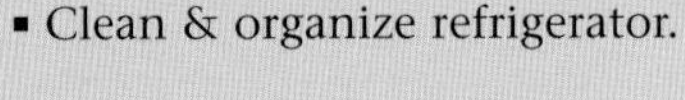 ▪ Clean & organize refrigerator. | ▪ Make Chilled Cucumber-Curry Soup.<br>▪ Prepare Vodka-Spiked Tomato Sauce.<br>▪ Shred cheese for Gougères.<br>▪ Make pastry cream for cake.<br>▪ Prepare Strawberry-Rhubarb filling for cake. |
| Staging  | ▪ Sketch a diagram of table set-up & placement of items. Plan seating arrangements.<br>▪ Plan & purchase tableware & decorations.<br>▪ Borrow or purchase needed cookware & serving dishes.<br>▪ Schedule housecleaner or childcare if needed.<br>▪ Ask friends or family for specific help if needed.<br>▪ Decide what to wear. | ▪ Iron tablecloths & napkins.<br>▪ Gather, wash, & polish serving platters, utensils, dishes, & glassware.<br>▪ Set table with dinner plates, silver or flatware, glasses, salt shakers, & pepper grinders. Cover with another tablecloth or sheet to keep clean.<br>▪ Confirm plans with outside help. |

*Though this is certainly a full-scale meal, much of the work is spread out over the preceding week, and you will have time to savor the joys of cooking. These are just guidelines to help your party go as smoothly as possible. Remember that you are not bound to follow these precisely. Have fun!*

| DAY BEFORE EVENT | DAY OF EVENT | LAST TWO HOURS |
| --- | --- | --- |
| | ▪ Assist guests with last-minute phone calls & requests. | |
| ▪ Purchase fish and flowers. | ▪ Purchase last-minute items: ice. | |
| ▪ Portion halibut.<br>▪ Chop onion, garlic, & herbs for rice pilaf.<br>▪ Make Almond Crème Anglaise.<br>▪ Begin Basque Cake; do not bake. | ▪ Bake Basque Cake. | ▪ Prepare Herbed Basmati Rice Pilaf, hold warm.<br><br>**BEFORE SERVING:**<br>▪ Warm Vodka-Tomato Sauce.<br>▪ Grill halibut.<br>▪ Make Asparagus with Lemon Bay Shrimp & Brown Butter.<br>▪ Make Gougères. |
| ▪ Chill sparkling wines, white wines, & beer.<br>▪ Set out dinner plates, tableware, & napkins. | ▪ Prepare coffee maker. Set coffee/tea service on tray.<br>▪ Do final cleaning of kitchen & bathroom.<br>▪ Set after dinner drinks & glasses on service tray. | ▪ Try to relax - take a 20 minute siesta or do some leisurely reading.<br>▪ Move pets to safe places.<br>▪ Feed children snacks.<br>▪ Shower, dress, & prepare yourself for the party!<br>▪ Open red wine.<br>▪ Pour juice into pitcher.<br>▪ Pour creamer into pitcher.<br>▪ Light candles.<br>▪ Put on music.<br>▪ Arrange food & drinks on buffet or table. |

# Gougères

*These cheesy, buttery egg puffs are perfect for the cocktail hour.*

¼ cup (60 ml) whole milk

¼ cup (60 ml) water

4 tablespoons (50 g) unsalted butter

½ teaspoon granulated sugar

¼ teaspoon kosher or sea salt

Pinch cayenne pepper

Pinch ground nutmeg

⅔ cup (100 g) all-purpose flour

2 large eggs

1 cup (4 ounces/100 g) finely shredded Gruyère cheese

1 egg

*makes about three dozen*

**EARLY PREPARATION:**

- Finely grate cheese. Refrigerate.

**PROCEDURE:**

Preheat oven to 400°F (200°C). Lightly butter or line a cookie sheet with parchment. Combine milk with water, butter, sugar, salt, cayenne, and nutmeg in a large saucepan. Bring to a boil. Remove pan from heat and add flour. Stir mixture with a wooden spoon until it forms a thick, smooth, paste-like batter. Cook for about 1 minute, stirring constantly. Scrape the batter into a large bowl and add the 2 eggs 1 at a time, incorporating each egg well. Blend in cheese.

Using a pastry bag without a tip or 2 small spoons, pipe or spoon slightly rounded tablespoons of batter onto prepared cookie sheet, spacing them 1 inch (2.5 cm) apart. Lightly beat the remaining egg and brush onto tops of the gougères. Bake for about 18 minutes, or until puffed and golden, rotating the pan halfway through the baking time. Serve warm.

# *Chilled Cucumber-Curry Soup*

3 tablespoons olive oil

1 large yellow onion, sliced into ¼ inch slices

¾ teaspoon curry powder

½ teaspoon kosher or sea salt

¼ teaspoon ground white pepper

6 cucumbers, peeled, seeded, and roughly chopped

3 cups (700 ml) chicken broth

2 tablespoons fresh lemon juice

2 cups (475 ml) heavy cream

3 tablespoons minced fresh dill, divided

*serves eight*

**PROCEDURE:**

Heat olive oil over medium heat in a large heavy saucepan. Add onions. Cook 2 to 3 minutes and add curry powder, salt, and white pepper. Cook another 2 to 3 minutes, stirring occasionally. Add cucumbers and cook for approximately 5 minutes. Add chicken broth and lemon juice and simmer for 8 to 10 minutes.

Purée soup, in batches, using a blender or food processor. Add soup back to saucepan and stir in heavy cream. Simmer for 5 minutes. Add 1 tablespoon of dill and remove from heat. Chill.

Taste and add more salt and pepper if needed before serving. Garnish with the remaining 2 tablespoons fresh dill.

# *Grilled Halibut Fillet with Vodka-Spiked Tomato Sauce*

*Salmon or sea bass are also delicious fish choices for this recipe!*

**SAUCE**

6 vine-ripened tomatoes

2 tablespoons tomato paste

2 tablespoons vodka

1 teaspoon prepared horseradish

2 tablespoons sherry vinegar

1 teaspoon kosher or sea salt

¼ teaspoon ground white pepper

½ teaspoon hot pepper sauce

4 tablespoons unsalted butter, room temperature, cut into 1 inch (2.5 cm) pieces

**HALIBUT**

1 (3 pound/1.35 kg) fresh halibut fillet, skinned, trimmed and portioned into 8 equal pieces, about 6 ounces (175 g) each

2 tablespoons olive oil

2 teaspoons kosher or sea salt

1 recipe Sauce (above)

*serves eight*

**EARLY PREPARATION:**

- Portion fish into 8 pieces. Refrigerate.

**PROCEDURE:**

**SAUCE**

Core and cut tomatoes in half horizontally. Squeeze out seeds and rough chop tomatoes into large pieces. Purée in a blender and strain through a fine sieve pressing firmly on tomatoes to extract as much juice as possible. Place the juice in a bowl and whisk in tomato paste, vodka, horseradish, vinegar, salt, white pepper, and hot pepper sauce. Reserve sauce until ready to serve.

To serve, slowly warm sauce on low heat. Whisk in butter. Serve immediately.

**HALIBUT**

Preheat grill to medium high.

Lightly oil both sides of fish and sprinkle with salt. Place fish on grill for approximately 3 minutes per side. (This will vary with the type of fish and how thick the pieces are.)

While fish is on the grill, warm sauce and whisk in butter.

Spoon 3 tablespoons of sauce on each dinner plate and place grilled halibut on top of sauce.

# *Herbed Basmati Rice Pilaf*

2 tablespoons olive oil

½ cup (100 g) minced onion

2 cloves garlic, minced

3 cups (600 g) basmati rice, rinsed

4 cups (950 ml) chicken broth

¼ teaspoon kosher or sea salt

¼ teaspoon ground white pepper

1 teaspoon minced fresh thyme

1 teaspoon minced fresh sage

*serves eight*

**EARLY PREPARATION:**

- Mince onion.
- Mince garlic.
- Mince thyme and sage.

**PROCEDURE:**

Preheat oven to 350°F (180°C).

Heat olive oil in a large ovenproof sauté pan with ovenproof lid. Add onion and then garlic. Add rinsed rice and stir to coat rice with oil. Lower heat and cook for about 2 minutes, stirring constantly. Stir in chicken broth, salt, and white pepper and bring to a simmer. Cover. Place sauté pan in oven. Bake for 15 minutes.

Sprinkle rice with thyme and sage. Cover and bake another 5 minutes. Remove pan from oven (do not take off lid). Let rice rest, covered, for 10 minutes. Fluff with fork before serving.

# *Steamed Asparagus with Lemon Bay Shrimp and Brown Butter*

- 2½ pounds fresh asparagus
- 2 teaspoons fresh lemon juice
- 2 teaspoons dry sherry
- 4 tablespoons unsalted butter
- ¾ pound (350 g) cooked bay shrimp
- Pinch kosher or sea salt
- Pinch black pepper

**CHEFS' TIP:**

*Properly browned butter adds such an interesting flavor to foods. When the butter just starts to change color it is time to take it off the heat. Because it is so intensely hot at this point it will continue to cook. If brown butter turns to black butter, the flavor goes from wonderfully nutty to bitter and burned.*

*serves eight*

**PROCEDURE:**

Snap off and discard ends of asparagus and wash well. Put into large sauté or saucepan with ½ inch (1 cm) water and a sprinkling of salt on top. Cover tightly and simmer over medium heat until stalks are tender, about 2 to 3 minutes. Drain water and put asparagus on a warm serving platter in a warm spot. (The oven on a very low setting is perfect if your platter is ovenproof; otherwise cover with foil and keep on top of the stove.)

Put pan back on stove and add lemon juice and sherry. When lemon juice and sherry have almost completely evaporated, add butter and swirl pan. Keep cooking for about 1 more minute until butter starts to turn brown and gives off a nutty odor. Toss in shrimp and heat just to warm. Stir in salt and pepper. Turn off heat and top asparagus with the lemon bay shrimp and brown butter mixture.

# *Basque Strawberry-Rhubarb Cake*

**PASTRY CREAM**

¾ cup (175 ml) whole milk

1 egg

2 egg yolks

¼ cup (50 g) granulated sugar

¼ cup (40 g) all-purpose flour, sifted

1 tablespoon light rum

**FILLING**

1½ cups (350 g) chopped rhubarb (½ inch/1 cm pieces)

⅔ cup (60 g) light brown sugar

1 pint (450 g) strawberries, hulled and halved

¾ teaspoon ground cardamom

Pinch kosher or sea salt

*serves twelve*

**PROCEDURE:**

**PASTRY CREAM**

In a medium saucepan, bring milk to a boil and turn heat to very low. In a medium bowl, combine egg, egg yolks, sugar, and flour and whisk until well combined. Temper the egg mix by adding a third of the hot milk while whisking constantly. Whisk the tempered egg mix into the remaining milk in saucepan and place over medium heat, whisking constantly, for about 6 minutes or until it is thick and pudding-like. Remove from heat and stir in rum. Refrigerate for 2 hours.

**FILLING**

Cook rhubarb and brown sugar in a saucepan over very low heat until rhubarb begins to release moisture and sugar melts. Add strawberries, cardamom, and salt, and raise the heat to medium. Cook until jam-like, stirring often, about 30 to 35 minutes. Remove from heat and refrigerate.

*Continued on next page.*

# Basque Strawberry-Rhubarb Cake

*Continued from previous page.*

**CAKE**

3 sticks (1½ cups/350 g) unsalted butter, room temperature

¾ cup (150 g) granulated sugar

½ teaspoon salt

1 egg

2 egg yolks

2½ cups (560 g) cake flour, sifted

**GLAZE**

1 egg, lightly beaten

1 tablespoon milk

**PROCEDURE:**

**CAKE**

Beat butter, sugar, and salt in bowl of an electric mixer on high for 5 minutes. Add egg and beat on high for 1 minute. Add 1 egg yolk and beat on high for 1 minute. Add other egg yolk and beat on high for 1 minute. Add cake flour and stir just to incorporate. Cover the batter and refrigerate for 2 hours.

Coat the inside of an 8 inch (20 cm) springform pan with nonstick spray. Turn the batter onto a lightly floured work surface. Divide the batter into 2 unequal pieces, one about ⅔ of the batter and the other about ⅓ of batter. Flatten the large piece with floured hands to 1-inch (2.5 cm) thickness and use it to line the bottom and sides of the springform pan. Come up the sides of the pan about 1 inch (2.5 cm). Batter will be very soft and sticky. It is a little difficult to work with, but well worth it! Spread filling onto batter and top with cooled pastry cream. On a floured board with floured hands, flatten out the remaining batter to 1½-inch (4 cm) thickness and place on top of pastry cream. Seal the edges.

**GLAZE**

Combine egg and milk and brush on the top of the cake. Refrigerate for 2 hours.

Preheat oven to 375°F (190°C). Bake on a sheet pan for 50 minutes, or until golden brown. Cool completely at room temperature. Serve with Almond Crème Anglaise (next page).

# *Almond Crème Anglaise*

6 egg yolks

⅓ cup (30 g) granulated sugar

2 cups (475 ml) half-and-half

1 teaspoon almond extract

*makes about three cups*

**PROCEDURE:**

Combine egg yolks and sugar in the bowl of a mixer. Beat with whip attachment until thick and light.

Scald half-and-half in a medium saucepan With mixer running on low speed, very gradually pour half-and-half into the yolk mixture. Pour mixture back into saucepan and heat slowly, stirring constantly until it thickens enough to coat the back of a spoon, about 185°F (85°C). Immediately remove from heat and pour through a mesh strainer into a clean stainless steel or glass bowl. Stir in almond extract.

Serve warm, or chill for later use.

# *Spring/Summer Formal Dinner* *shopping list*

*This is a complete list of ingredients you will need to make all the recipes in this menu, along with the quantity you will need for each ingredient. The menus are designed to feed a gathering of eight. If increasing or decreasing any recipes be certain to adjust quantities on the shopping list. Check your pantry before shopping, as you may already have enough of many of these items.*

### PRODUCE

- ☐ Asparagus (2½ lbs./1 kg)
- ☐ Cucumbers (6)
- ☐ Garlic (1 head)
- ☐ Lemons, for juice (2)
- ☐ Onion, yellow (1 large + 1 medium)
- ☐ Rhubarb (1½ cups/350 g)
- ☐ Strawberries (1 pint/450 g)
- ☐ Tomatoes, vine-ripened (6)

### HERBS

- ☐ Dill, fresh (1 Tbs.)
- ☐ Sage, fresh (1 tsp.)
- ☐ Thyme, fresh (1 tsp.)

### DAIRY/EGGS

- ☐ Butter, unsalted (1¼ lbs./500 g)
- ☐ Gruyère cheese (4 oz./100 g)
- ☐ Half-and-half (2 cups/475 ml)
- ☐ Heavy cream (2 cups/475 ml)
- ☐ Milk, whole (1¼ cups/270 ml)
- ☐ Eggs, large (16 )

### FISH/SEAFOOD

- ☐ Halibut (3 lbs./1.35 kg fillet or 8 x 6 oz./175 g)
- ☐ Shrimp, cooked bay (¾ lb./350 g)

### BAKING GOODS/SPICES

- ☐ Almond extract (1 tsp.)
- ☐ Cardamom, ground (3 tsp.)
- ☐ Cayenne pepper (pinch)
- ☐ Curry powder (¾ tsp.)
- ☐ Nutmeg, ground (pinch)

### CANNED GOODS

- ☐ Chicken broth (56 oz./2 l)
- ☐ Tomato paste (2 Tbs.)

### CONDIMENTS

- ☐ Horseradish, prepared (1 tsp.)
- ☐ Sherry vinegar (2 Tbs.)
- ☐ Hot pepper sauce (½ tsp.)

### DRY GOODS

- ☐ Rice, basmati (3 cups/600 g)

### PANTRY STAPLES

- ☐ Flour, all-purpose white (1 cup/160 g)
- ☐ Flour, cake (2½ cups/560 g)
- ☐ Oil, olive (7 Tbs.)
- ☐ Pepper, black
- ☐ Pepper, white
- ☐ Salt, kosher or sea
- ☐ Sugar, light brown (⅔ cup/60 g)
- ☐ Sugar, white granulated (1⅓ cups/230 g)

### LIQUOR

- ☐ Rum, light (1 Tbs.)
- ☐ Sherry, dry (2 tsp.)
- ☐ Vodka (2 Tbs.)

### WINE

- ☐ Sparkling wine, blanc de blancs
- ☐ Chardonnay, Sauvignon Blanc
- ☐ Ice wine
- ☐ Pinot Noir, Syrah, or Merlot

### SUPPLIES

- ☐ Parchment cooking paper (optional)

# *spring/summer dessert buffet*

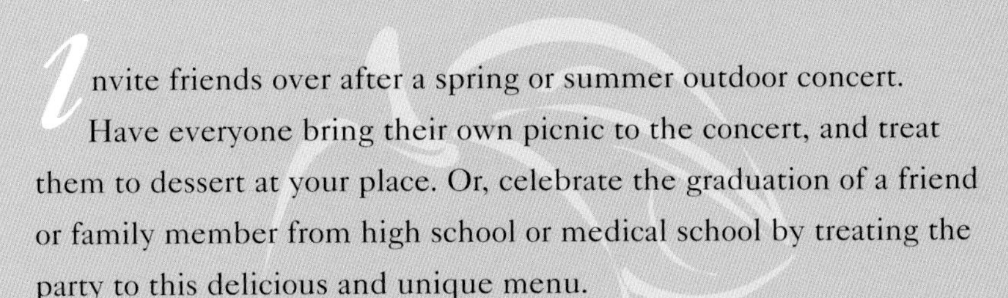

Invite friends over after a spring or summer outdoor concert. Have everyone bring their own picnic to the concert, and treat them to dessert at your place. Or, celebrate the graduation of a friend or family member from high school or medical school by treating the party to this delicious and unique menu.

This menu uses wonderful spring and summer strawberries and peaches. Seek out strawberries still on the vine to dip in chocolate or to drop in a glass for bubbly sparkling wine. Vanilla bean ice cream is fantastic with Warm Chocolate Cakes. Purchasing the ice cream reduces your time in the kitchen. Look for a high-quality vanilla bean ice cream with a homemade taste—not all ice creams are created equal. Caramel Cake is melt-in-your-mouth decadence, and Strawberry-Mascarpone Tarts provide a tangy contrast to the other menu items.

This indulgent occasion calls for an extra dry sparkling wine or Late Harvest Riesling.

SPRING/SUMMER

# Dessert Buffet Menu

*Caramel Cake*

PAGE 150-151

*Strawberry-Mascarpone Tarts*

PAGE 152

*Individual Warm Chocolate Cakes*

PAGE 153

*Vanilla Bean Ice Cream*

*(Purchase)*

*Baked Almond-Filled Peaches*

PAGE 154

BEVERAGE SUGGESTION

*Extra Dry Sparkling Wine*

*Late Harvest Riesling*

*Photo: Strawberry-Mascarpone Tarts*

# Dessert Buffet
## *planning guide*

| | ADVANCE PREPARATIONS | PREP TIME *(2 to 3 Days Ahead)* |
|---|---|---|
| Hospitality | ▪ Create guest list. Call or send invitations.<br>▪ Provide directions if needed.<br>▪ Print shopping list & menu from www.seahillpress.com website. | ▪ Call any guests who have not responded.<br>▪ Talk to neighbors & plan parking arrangements. |
| Shopping  | ▪ Review list of ingredients. | ▪ Purchase beverages & groceries (not fruit). |
|  Food Preparation | 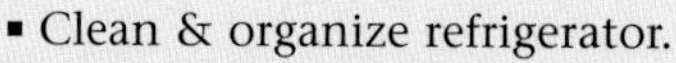 ▪ Clean & organize refrigerator. | ▪ Make filling for peaches. Refrigerate.<br>▪ Prepare caramel sauce for cake. Refrigerate. |
| Staging  | ▪ Sketch a diagram of table set-up & placement of items. Plan seating arrangements.<br>▪ Plan & purchase tableware & decorations.<br>▪ Borrow or purchase needed cookware & serving dishes.<br>▪ Schedule house cleaner or childcare if needed.<br>▪ Decide what to wear. | ▪ Gather, wash, & polish serving platters, utensils, dishes, & glassware.<br>▪ Cover items with plastic wrap or tablecloth to keep clean. |

*Since so much has been done ahead of time for this menu you'll have time to clean up the kitchen while your house fills with the aroma of chocolate cake baking in the oven. What a delightful menu to serve! Made even better by the joy and ease of preparation. These are just guidelines to help your party go as smoothly as possible. Remember that you are not bound to follow these precisely. Have fun!*

| DAY BEFORE EVENT | DAY OF EVENT | LAST TWO HOURS |
|---|---|---|
| ▪ Assist guests with last-minute questions & requests. | | |
| ▪ Purchase strawberries, peaches, & ice cream. | ▪ Purchase last-minute items: flowers & ice. | |
| ▪ Prepare dough for Strawberry-Mascarpone Tarts. Store loosely covered at room temperature.<br>▪ Prepare filling for Strawberry-Mascarpone Tarts. Refrigerate. | ▪ Finish and bake Caramel Cake.<br>▪ Fill peaches.<br>▪ Make batter for Individual Warm Chocolate Cakes. Refrigerate in individual souflé cups. | ▪ Finish Strawberry-Mascarpone Tarts.<br>**BEFORE SERVING:**<br>▪ Bake peaches.<br>▪ Bake Individual Warm Chocolate Cakes.<br>▪ Remove ice cream from freezer 15 minutes before serving. |
| ▪ Set up serving tables with pedestals, tablecloths, & decorations.<br>▪ Clean house. Iron tablecloths & napkins.<br>▪ Confirm arrangements with outside help.<br>▪ Set-up buffet & seating areas. | ▪ Chill sparkling wines & white wines.<br>▪ Set out dinner plates, tableware, & napkins.<br>▪ Prepare coffee maker. Set coffee/tea service on tray.<br>▪ Do final cleaning of kitchen & bathroom. | ▪ Try to relax - take a 20 minute siesta or do some leisurely reading.<br>▪ Move pets to safe places.<br>▪ Feed snacks to young children.<br>▪ Shower, dress, & prepare yourself for the party!<br>▪ Pour creamer into pitcher.<br>▪ Light candles.<br>▪ Put on music.<br>▪ Arrange food & drinks on buffet or table. |

# *Caramel Cake*

*I think of this as one of those died-and-went-to-heaven cakes that makes your mouth water at just the thought of it! The caramel sauce is so satisfying and creamy that you may find yourself searching for excuses to make it. Not to worry, it is delicious as a dip for sliced apples, an ice cream topping, or a sauce for such desserts as pound cake or bread pudding. For a little variety, you can add a tablespoon of whisky, brandy, or flavored liqueur.*

**CARAMEL SAUCE**

2 cups (475 ml) heavy cream

1¼ cups (250 g) granulated sugar

*serves twelve*

**EARLY PREPARATION:**

- Prepare caramel sauce in advance. Refrigerate.

**PROCEDURE:**

**CARAMEL SAUCE**

Bring heavy cream to a boil in a medium saucepan. Turn heat to very low and keep warm.

Warm sugar in a heavy, medium saucepan over medium heat. Leave undisturbed until sugar melts and begins to darken. Gently shake the pan to distribute sugar and to keep it from burning. When caramel is a dark amber color, remove it from heat and carefully add hot cream, stirring constantly with a wooden spoon. The caramel will bubble and steam so be very careful! Keep caramel over heat, stirring until it is completely melted and without lumps. Set aside to cool.

**STORAGE:**

Measure out 1 cup to add to caramel cake if making cake right away, otherwise refrigerate any that is not being used immediately.

*Continued on next page.*

# Caramel Cake

*Continued from previous page.*

**CARAMEL CAKE**

1½ sticks (¾ cup/175 g) unsalted butter, room temperature

1¼ cups (250 g) brown sugar

4 eggs, room temperature

1 teaspoon vanilla extract

2 cups (320 g) all-purpose flour

1½ teaspoons baking powder

¼ teaspoon kosher or sea salt

1 recipe Caramel Sauce, divided (previous page)

**PROCEDURE:**

**CARAMEL CAKE**

Heat oven to 325°F (165°C). Grease and flour a 12-cup Bundt™ pan. With an electric mixer, beat butter and brown sugar until fluffy. Beat in eggs, 1 at a time, waiting until each is incorporated before adding the next. Add vanilla to the butter mixture. Sift together flour, baking powder, and salt and then gently but thoroughly fold the dry ingredients into the butter mixture alternately with the 1 cup of reserved caramel, beginning and ending with the dry ingredients.

Pour the batter into the prepared pan and bake until a skewer comes out clean, about 40 minutes. Set on a rack for about 10 minutes and then turn cake over onto rack and cool completely.

Bring the rest of the caramel sauce to room temperature. When the cake is cool, glaze it by drizzling half of the remaining caramel sauce over the top. Save the rest to serve with the cake and purchased vanilla bean ice cream.

# Strawberry-Mascarpone Tarts

**DOUGH**

1½ sticks (¾ cup /175 g) unsalted butter

2 cups (320 g) all-purpose flour

½ cup (100 g) powdered sugar

Pinch kosher or sea salt

**MASCARPONE FILLING**

2 cups (475 ml) mascarpone

½ cup (50 g) brown sugar

2 teaspoons vanilla

2 tablespoons milk

2 pints (900 g) strawberries

Fresh mint sprigs, for garnish

*serves eight to ten*

**EARLY PREPARATION:**

- Prepare dough in advance. Store loosely covered at room temperature.
- Prepare filling in advance. Refrigerate.

**PROCEDURE:**

**DOUGH**

Place all ingredients in food processor or mixer and process until dough comes together in a ball. Roll out to ¼-inch (5 mm) thick or simply press into a 10-inch (25.5 cm) well-greased tart pan or 8 individual serving size tart pans. Chill for 30 minutes.

Preheat oven to 350°F (180°C). Bake directly on oven rack, until dough just begins to brown, about 7 minutes. Remove from oven and cool slightly. Remove dough from pan(s) while still slightly warm.

**MASCARPONE FILLING**

Blend mascarpone with brown sugar, vanilla, and milk. Spoon filling in tart shell or 8 individual shells and spread evenly with an off-set spatula or back of spoon. Slice strawberries ¼-inch (5 mm) thick and fan over the filling, starting with the outside and working in a circular pattern towards the center until the entire surface is covered. Garnish with a sprig of fresh mint.

# *Individual Warm Chocolate Cakes*

*These are delicious served warm with vanilla bean ice cream.*

1½ sticks (¾ cup/175 g) unsalted butter

9 ounces (285 g) bittersweet chocolate

3 eggs

3 egg yolks

⅓ cup (30 g) sugar

2 teaspoons vanilla

¼ teaspoon kosher or sea salt

3 tablespoons all-purpose flour

*serves eight*

**PROCEDURE:**

Butter generously and flour 8 (6 ounce/170 g) ramekins (small soufflé dishes).

Melt butter and chocolate in a double boiler over low heat. Whisk until smooth. Beat eggs with egg yolks, sugar, vanilla, and salt with an electric mixer at high speed, until thick and pale yellow in color. Fold egg mixture into chocolate mixture. Stir in flour. Pour or spoon batter into prepared ramekins.

Refrigerate batter-filled ramekins for up to several hours, if desired. Bring back to room temperature before baking.

Place cakes in oven on a cookie sheet and bake for 9 to 12 minutes, until sides are set but center is still very loose. Take out of oven and let cakes rest for 1 minute. Cover each cake with an inverted plate and carefully turn over. Let sit for just a few seconds and then pull ramekin off. Serve immediately.

# *Baked Almond-Filled Peaches*

**ALMOND FILLING**

½ cup (50 g) sliced almonds, lightly toasted and ground to a fine powder

3 tablespoons unsalted butter

2 tablespoons light brown sugar

1 tablespoon amaretto liqueur

or 1 teaspoon almond extract

⅛ teaspoon kosher or sea salt

1 egg white

2 tablespoons all-purpose flour

**BAKED PEACHES**

4 peaches, ripe but firm (peel if desired)

1 recipe Almond Filling

2 cups (475 ml) Late Harvest Riesling or other sweet dessert wine

*serves eight*

**EARLY PREPARATION:**

- Prepare almond filling in advance. Refrigerate for up to 2 days.

**PROCEDURE:**

**ALMOND FILLING**

Toast and grind almonds to a fine powder.

Beat almonds, butter, and sugar together in an electric mixer until light and fluffy. Add amaretto or almond extract and salt. Add egg white and flour and beat until well combined.

**BAKED PEACHES**

Peel peaches if desired. Halve and remove pit.

Preheat oven to 350°F (180°C). In a saucepan, bring wine to a simmer and turn off heat.

Evenly distribute the almond filling among peaches, mounding it where pit had been.

Place peach halves in a baking dish (stuffed-side up) and pour wine around them. Bake until peaches are tender and hot and filling is light brown on top, about 10 minutes. Transfer peaches to a serving platter using a slotted spoon.

Pour wine back into saucepan on medium heat and reduce by half, about 10 minutes. Drizzle reduced wine over peaches and serve.

# *Spring/Summer Dessert Buffet* *shopping list*

*This is a complete list of ingredients you will need to make all the recipes in this menu, along with the quantity you will need for each ingredient. The menus are designed to feed a gathering of eight. If increasing or decreasing any recipes be certain to adjust quantities on the shopping list. Check your pantry before shopping, as you may already have enough of many of these items.*

### PRODUCE

- ☐ Peaches, ripe but firm (4)
- ☐ Strawberries (3 pints/1.35 kg)

### HERBS

- ☐ Mint sprigs (about 12)

### DAIRY/EGGS

- ☐ Butter, unsalted (1¼ lbs./500 g)
- ☐ Heavy cream (2 cups/475 ml)
- ☐ Milk (2 Tbs.)
- ☐ Mascarpone cheese (2 cups/475 ml)
- ☐ Eggs (7)

### BAKING GOODS

- ☐ Almonds, sliced (½ cup/50 g)
- ☐ Almond extract (1 tsp.) (or 1 Tbs. amaretto liqueur)
- ☐ Bittersweet chocolate (9 oz./285 g)
- ☐ Vanilla extract (5 tsp.)

### PANTRY STAPLES

- ☐ Baking powder (1½ tsp.)
- ☐ Flour, all-purpose (5 cups/800 g)
- ☐ Salt, kosher or sea
- ☐ Sugar, brown (1¾ cups/300 g)
- ☐ Sugar, granulated white (1¾ cups/280 g)
- ☐ Sugar, light brown (2 Tbs.)
- ☐ Sugar, powdered (½ cup/100 g)

### FROZEN FOODS

- ☐ Vanilla bean ice cream (½ gal./2 l)

### LIQUOR

- ☐ Amaretto liqueur (1 Tbs.) (or 1 tsp. almond extract)

### WINE

- ☐ Sparkling wine, extra dry
- ☐ Late Harvest Riesling (2 cups/475 ml) or other sweet dessert wine

# Index



*Page numbers in boldface indicate photos.*

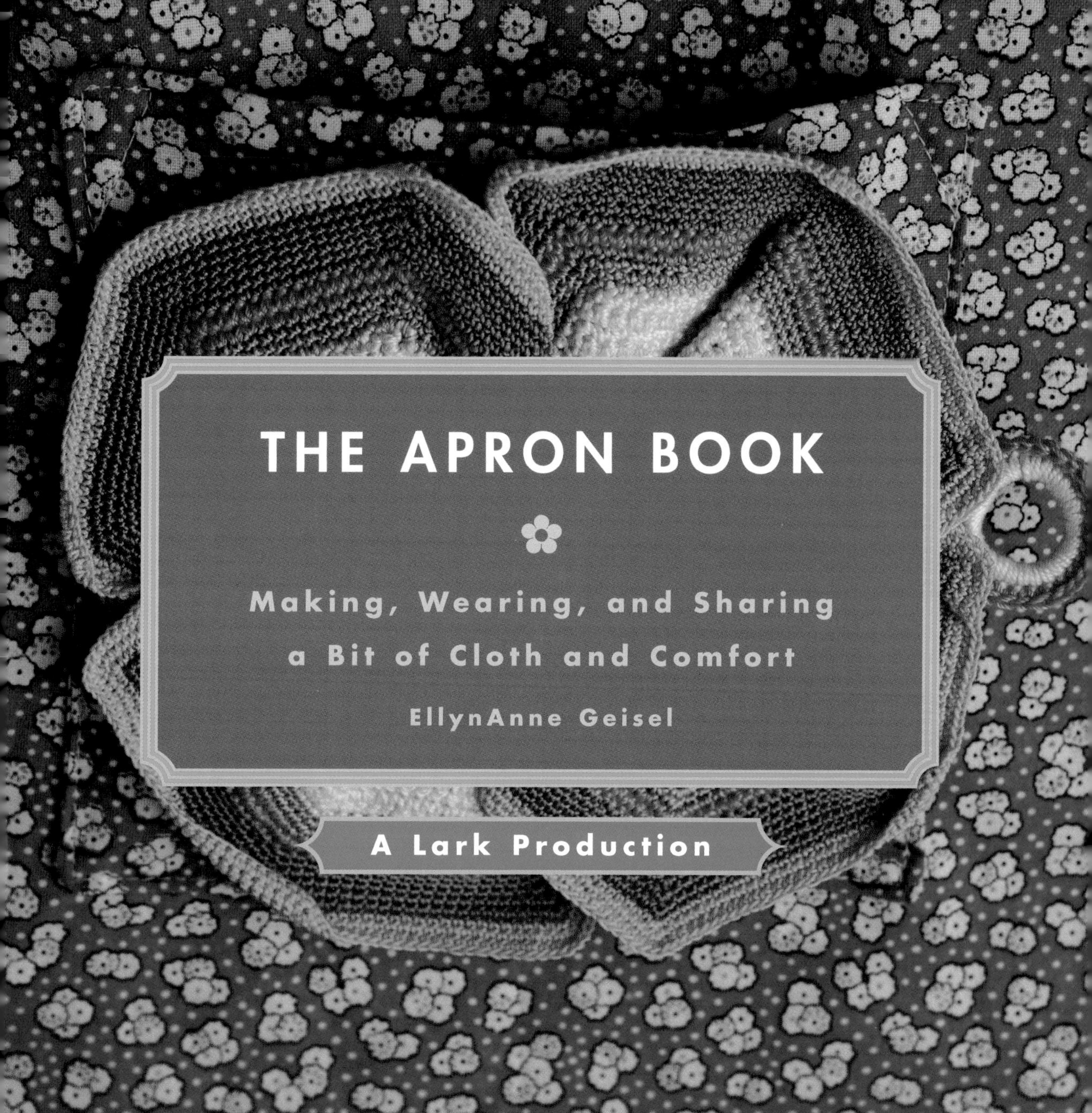


Andrews McMeel
Publishing, LLC
Kansas City

*To Hank, my prince charming*

## THE APRON BOOK

Copyright © 2006 by EllynAnne Geisel. All rights reserved. Printed in China. No part of this book may be used or reproduced in any manner whatsoever without written permission except in the case of reprints in the context of reviews. For information, write Andrews McMeel Publishing, LLC, an Andrews McMeel Universal company, 4520 Main Street, Kansas City, Missouri 64111.

08 09 10 WKT 10 9 8 7

Library of Congress Cataloging-in-Publication Data

The apron book: making, wearing, and sharing a bit of cloth and comfort/[edited] by EllynAnne Geisel.
p. cm.
ISBN-13: 978-0-7407-6181-2
ISBN-10: 0-7407-6181-1
I. Geisel, EllynAnne.

TT546.5.G45 2006
391.4'4—dc22

2006042903

Book design by Diane Marsh

www.andrewsmcmeel.com

**ATTENTION: SCHOOLS AND BUSINESSES**

Andrews McMeel books are available at quantity discounts with bulk purchase for educational, business, or sales promotional use. For information, please write to: Special Sales Department, Andrews McMeel Publishing, LLC, 4520 Main Street, Kansas City, Missouri 64111.